The Memory Gardener

By: Mustafa Nejem

PROLOGUE

"The Memory Gardener", In a reality where memories can be cultivated akin to flowers, Joseph, a skilled memory gardener, helps individuals reconstruct lost memories resulting from trauma or aging. The story unfolds as Marlon, a client, approaches Joseph with an unusual request: to cultivate a memory linked to a decades-old crime. Joseph becomes entangled in a moral dilemma, torn between honoring his client's wishes and facing pressure from authorities eager to exploit these memory-gardens as evidence.

.

CONTENTS

Chapter 1

The Garden of Remembrance

Joseph, a charming expert memory gardener. His enthusiasm overflows as he shares heartwarming stories that paint the delicacy of memories. He knows how a loving smile can fade into the haze of forgetfulness or how the sparkle in a child's eyes fades when forgetting a special moment. His stories lead us towards those small details that, despite their apparent insignificance, are the pillars of memories shaping people's lives. They speak of those moments that, when forgotten, become lost fragments in the vast landscape of each person's memory, marking the importance of every glimmer of joy and every caress of love in our lives.

He is fully committed to his task, diving deep into the twists and turns of the human mind to find lost memories. It's as if he's an artist, meticulously putting together tiny pieces of the past.

He's like a detective, searching for clues in the intricate pathways of memory. His dedication is unwavering as he pieces together each fragment, almost like a puzzle master assembling scattered pieces to reveal a complete picture. Every step he takes is deliberate, slowly constructing a cohesive and comprehensive narrative from the fragments he uncovers, showing his meticulous and thorough approach to his work.

His work isn't just about memories; it's about touching lives. He brings back stories that tug at the heart, showing how crucial his work is for those who lost parts of their history. Each detail he reconstructs is like finding a precious gem, shedding light in the forgotten shadows of time. His dedication doesn't just rebuild memories; it restores hope and meaning to those whose stories were lost. He's not just piecing together moments; he's rekindling the very essence of people's lives.

Joseph approaches the forgotten memories with a serene touch, as if his calmness has magic. He's like an artist reviving faded paintings, but his canvas is the human mind. Every memory he rekindles isn't just a picture; it's a garden bursting with life. He doesn't just recall moments; he paints them with vibrant colors and fragrances that stir feelings. Each memory he nurtures isn't just a recollection; it's a legacy, a tale that reshapes and completes those who've lost a part of themselves. His work isn't just about remembering; it's about rekindling the very essence of who people are.

It is as if he weaves threads of time, rescuing moments to return them as treasures to their owners, illuminating their lives with glimpses of a past that seemed to be buried.

There is a mixture of humility and a touch of satisfaction as he talks about his work: the power to regain vitality in life, to reunite the bonds that time and challenges have worn away.

He speaks with a deep conviction, almost ingrained in his being, about how these gardens of memories go beyond just being a job; He sees them as a true vocation that has the purpose of healing wounds in the heart and safeguarding the most essential of what is human: memory. It's as if he fervently believes that by returning those lost pieces of history, he's restoring more than just memories; It is restoring the very essence of people.

Chapter 2

The Mystery Shopper

In a quiet moment, wrapped in a mist that made the day feel hushed and dim, Joseph's peaceful home stood adorned by a vibrant garden that burst with colors. Suddenly, a persistent knock broke the tranquility. Joseph, eager to find the source, hurried to the door. Standing before him was Marlon, a man whose calmness contrasted with the intensity in his eyes. His gaze seemed to hold stories untold, as if he had glimpsed the deepest secrets of the world. In those eyes, an intricate blend of emotions swirled – pain mingled with an unyielding determination, a storm of feelings that twirled and danced within him. There was a sense of intrigue in the air, as if the meeting of these two souls marked the beginning of an unforeseen journey.

Joseph couldn't miss the mystery behind Marlon's arrival; it felt like an invisible charge filled the air. Marlon, despite his quiet demeanor, carried an intense urgency that echoed in every word he spoke. In hushed tones, filled with nervousness, Marlon revealed his challenging quest to reclaim a lost memory. This memory wasn't just a fleeting thought; it was a crucial piece that connected to a puzzling event from his past. The weight of his words hung in the room, painting a vivid picture of a story waiting to be unveiled, sparking curiosity about what lay hidden within Marlon's forgotten recollections.

In the gradual but pressing tale Marlon shared, Joseph sensed the heaviness of a memory slipping away, haunting Marlon deeply. It was a crucial part of his life story fading into the darkness of forgotten times, a connection that meant the world to him, now lost in the crevices of oblivion. Joseph could feel Marlon's yearning to retrieve this vital fragment, a bond that held immense significance in Marlon's personal history, buried beneath the passing of time.

This account carried the weight of Marlon's longing, painting a poignant picture of a cherished memory, fading away beyond reach, and the desperation to bring it back into the light.

Marlon's eyes held a deep sorrow that seemed to echo through Joseph's own feelings. In every glance, in each trace of pain, there lay an unspoken plea for support. Joseph sensed a whirlwind of emotions swirling within Marlon, a language of distress that everyone could understand, touching Joseph's heart deeply. It was like Marlon's silent plea, a cry that spoke volumes about inner struggles and worries. This connection, born from a single look, plunged Joseph into a world of shared feelings and a profound desire to offer solace and understanding. The empathy Joseph felt bridged their emotions, creating a powerful connection beyond words.

In the midst of uncertainty, Joseph felt an irresistible pull toward Marlon's enigmatic plea.

The shadows cloaking Marlon's request didn't deter Joseph; instead, they added to the mystery, enticing his interest. Marlon's urgency, the deep-rooted need to reclaim a piece of his past, ignited Joseph's natural inquisitiveness. It was a fusion of a thirst for discovery and an uncontainable urge to aid that propelled Joseph forward. He couldn't resist the call to assist, acknowledging the commitment ahead, foreseeing uncharted territories and unpredictable truths waiting to be unraveled. This blend of intrigue and a compassionate drive pushed Joseph to embrace the challenge with a determination to navigate unexplored territories and uncover the hidden fragments of Marlon's history.

After bidding farewell to Marlon, Joseph found solace within the comforting confines of his home, a space steeped in countless tales and memories. Here, in this familiar haven, he embarked on a journey of unraveling the riddle entwined with Marlon's past.

Fueled by an unwavering determination, Joseph treated the task as an exploration, venturing into the concealed recesses of Marlon's mind. Every stride he took within this intricate labyrinth of memories was purposeful, driven by an unrelenting commitment to unearth the elusive memory shrouded in the deepest crevices of Marlon's consciousness. With each step forward, Joseph embraced the challenge with resolute perseverance, navigating the intricacies of Marlon's narrative with the meticulousness of an explorer charting unknown territories, aiming to illuminate the obscured corners of Marlon's past.

In his study, Joseph was like a detective, diving deep into the details Marlon shared. He examined every tiny thing from their meeting—words, how Marlon moved, even the way he looked. All of it was super important, like pieces to a giant puzzle about Marlon's life. Joseph collected every photo and note, treating them like parts of a big mental game he was playing.

He sorted everything so carefully, trying to link them together to make sense of Marlon's whole story. With lots of patience and care, Joseph pieced together these fragments, hoping to unlock the hidden truth Marlon held.

Joseph's mind was like a super busy workshop where ideas mixed and tangled, especially when it came to Marlon's mystery. Every single day became this big guessing game, where Joseph tried to solve puzzles that felt unsolvable. His thoughts were all over the place, like a big dance, twisting and turning like tangled threads in his head. The feelings swirling around were like music in his house,

making everything feel so intense. It was as if his whole place was buzzing with curiosity, like there were hidden clues all around, and Joseph just couldn't stop looking for answers to unlock Marlon's forgotten memory.

Joseph's interest in Marlon's case was like a big mix of being super curious and feeling this rush to figure things out fast.

Whenever he talked to Marlon, it felt like diving into a pool of emotions. Marlon's stories were so intriguing, like secret messages being revealed to Joseph. He paid close attention, trying to connect all the dots like a pro. It was like Joseph was weaving an invisible web, linking every tiny bit of information Marlon shared. In a way, he was piecing together a puzzle made of Marlon's stories, trying to see the bigger picture hidden within.

Marlon's memories weren't just bits floating around; they were woven into a fabric of feelings and moments tied to this missing piece. Joseph wasn't just after finding a memory; he wanted to dig deep, to really get what made these memories matter so much. He wasn't only curious; he really cared about what these memories meant to people. He wanted to understand not just the forgotten bits, but the people themselves, to connect with the heart of why these memories held so much weight in their lives.

It was like peeling layers of an onion, trying to get to the core of what mattered most to them, beyond just the forgotten piece.

Every bit of information from Marlon was precious to Joseph, each tiny detail like a puzzle piece. The way Marlon talked, the things he didn't say, even his movements, were all clues for Joseph's mission. It wasn't just a job to him; it was a personal mission. Joseph felt deeply connected, like he was exploring what it means to really live, to understand the core of our existence. This wasn't about work; it was diving into life's mysteries, delving into what makes us human, and understanding the depth of our experiences. Every moment was a step into understanding life's essence, a journey beyond the boundaries of a regular job. In the quiet night, time moved slowly for Joseph as he delved into this puzzling world.

Each passing moment felt like it vanished into the dark, but to him, it was a chance to dig deeper into these memories. He felt like an adventurer exploring hidden corners of the mind, gathering every forgotten piece. These memories were like scattered puzzle parts, and Joseph, patiently, put them together. It was like assembling a complex puzzle, discovering how these pieces fit together, almost like they were dancing in a secret pattern that only he could decode. Each second was an opportunity to unlock another part of this intricate puzzle.

Joseph's journey seemed unending, days blending into weeks as he navigated the complexities of Marlon's thoughts. Each revelation felt like a small spark lighting up the shadows in Marlon's mind. But, strangely, with every discovery, more mysteries emerged, pulling Joseph further into the tangle of emotions and secrets tied to that past incident.

Each solution unearthed seemed to beckon more puzzles, drawing him deeper into the labyrinth of memories etched into Marlon's soul. It was as if every answer he found was a pathway leading to another riddle, revealing the intricate tapestry of memories interwoven within Marlon's very being. Joseph felt a deep urge to uncover the enigma surrounding Marlon, diving into every resource available to shed light on the obscured corners of this mystery. With each clue he unraveled, a new layer of emotion emerged, leading him into uncharted emotional depths. It was like stepping into a dark tunnel; every step forward brought more questions and a growing realization of the emotional complexity hidden within Marlon's story. Joseph's journey was not just about solving a puzzle; it was about navigating the emotional landscape Marlon carried, encountering complexities that went beyond mere facts or evidence, delving into the very heart of Marlon's emotional world.

Joseph's quest for Marlon's truth felt like peeling back layers of a mystery, revealing a world previously unseen. Each revelation was not a resolution but an introduction to more complexities. It was like entering a labyrinth where every new detail led to an emotional maze, making him realize that for every answer, more queries emerged. Each clue, while shedding light, also deepened the shadows, unraveling a tapestry of emotions interwoven in Marlon's history. With each step, Joseph found himself not just deciphering a story but navigating through a landscape of intertwined sentiments, unveiling the vastness of Marlon's concealed emotions and experiences.

In Joseph's quiet sanctuary, every photograph was a window into something far beyond forgotten moments. It wasn't just about restoring a memory; he felt the weight of how it could change not just Marlon's life, but his own too. Each photo, each scribbled note, held more than just stories; they were reflections of their intertwined destinies.

He saw in them not just past events but glimpses of the roads they walked, and maybe where they were heading. Every detail he discovered wasn't just another piece of history; it was a potential turning point, a puzzle piece that could reshape their stories and futures in unexpected ways.

Joseph's commitment to his task was more than just a job; it was a quest to untangle Marlon's enigmatic past. With each move closer to the truth, Joseph felt the weight of Marlon's emotions. Every emotion, every event from Marlon's life became a key, unlocking the doors to hidden memories. Each step forward wasn't just a discovery; it was like stepping into Marlon's world, understanding his joys, his sorrows, and the intricate layers of his past that shaped him. It was more than unraveling memories; it was trying to comprehend Marlon's very being, to see the world through his eyes and understand the complexities that governed his life's journey.

Joseph recognized that unearthing this lost memory wasn't just about finding clues; it was about handling each detail delicately, understanding the impact of each revelation on Marlon's life, and the weight it carried in reshaping his story.

Chapter 3

The Singular Assignment

In the midst of his usual peaceful routine, Joseph's home became a sanctuary where he nurtured memories. However, this sanctuary was unexpectedly stirred by Marlon's unanticipated return. This time, Marlon's countenance bore a shift, a transformation etched in deeper emotions. His face held a weightier burden, almost as if the shadows of his past had thickened since their last encounter. There was a palpable change in Marlon, an alteration that Joseph keenly perceived. The emotions etched across Marlon's face hinted at a stirring within, an unseen turmoil that had perhaps grown heavier with time.

Marlon began to open up to Joseph, a sign of increasing trust and vulnerability. His words, cautiously chosen yet brimming with anticipation, held a profound yearning. He shared a poignant desire—to unearth a memory deeply buried within his history. This particular memory, intertwined with a somber chapter from his past, carried a veil of mystery.

Through his cautious revelations, Marlon conveyed the delicate nature of this quest, seeking Joseph's guidance and support in navigating the shadows of this elusive recollection.

Marlon's disclosure stirred a mix of astonishment and wariness within Joseph. The gravity and significance of the plea shimmered in Marlon's eyes, mingled with a hint of intrigue. Joseph sensed the weightiness of the request and the profound implications hidden behind Marlon's gaze. Understanding the intricate nature of memory cultivation, Joseph recognized the task's complexity. He anticipated not only the challenge of his memory-crafting skills but also the uncharted terrain of uncertainties and unforeseen discoveries that lay ahead. It was as though Marlon's plea marked the beginning of an enigmatic journey fraught with intricate layers yet to be unveiled.

Joseph's mind was a canvas painted with caution, yet curiosity and resolve blended within him. He comprehended the weight and delicacy of the impending task.

It wasn't just about reconstructing memories; it was a potential journey into uncharted territories of revelations. He was aware that this undertaking wouldn't solely examine his prowess in memory restoration but might unfurl unforeseen truths. It was a tightrope walk between the known and the uncharted, a boundary-pushing venture in his role as a memory healer, where every step could uncover secrets hidden in the delicate fabric of forgotten recollections.

Joseph found himself at a critical juncture, balancing between the peculiar and the unfamiliar. Marlon's quest to unravel a memory linked to a hazy past presented an unparalleled challenge. The significance of Marlon's plea echoed with the weight of a history veiled in obscurity, concealing untold secrets he yearned to unearth and confront. This demand placed Joseph in unexplored realms, a domain where each move might unveil unforeseen revelations and disclose truths buried beneath layers of forgetfulness.

It was a delicate balance between the known and the concealed, marking Joseph's foray into uncharted territories of memory and discovery. The task before him held the potential to rewrite the narrative of Marlon's obscured past.

Joseph's role as a memory gardener blended the precision of science with the artistry of creativity, an interplay that defined his work. While each client's narrative carried its distinct significance, Marlon's request stood as an extraordinary challenge. It wasn't just another task; it was a journey into the depths of Marlon's consciousness, aiming to unearth a memory shrouded in the profound darkness of his past. This wasn't merely about applying technical prowess; it demanded an expedition into uncharted territories of the human psyche, traversing enigmatic pathways where uncertainty and the unexpected might prevail. It was a unique quest that required Joseph to wield not just expertise, but also an intuitive understanding of the human mind and its intricate complexities.

Marlon's revelations unveiled a cryptic puzzle for Joseph, who sensed the weight of responsibility in every word shared. Each detail from Marlon echoed like a beacon, illuminating hidden corners of a memory maze long obscured. Joseph realized this wasn't solely about retrieving a forgotten fragment; it meant navigating unforeseen implications for Marlon's life. It resembled setting sail into unexplored seas—each revelation not only unlocking new mysteries but also heralding unforeseen consequences. Every step forward in unraveling Marlon's past brought forth a cascade of inquiries and potential outcomes, making Joseph tread cautiously to ensure every revealed memory wouldn't disrupt Marlon's life irreparably.

Joseph found himself in a unique juncture, where the comfort of his home contrasted with the complexity of the task before him. This assignment wasn't solely about his technical prowess; it demanded an emotional and mental depth he hadn't encountered before.

It wasn't merely about recalling lost memories; it delved into the intricate maze of the human mind, potentially uncovering buried truths and unexplored facets of human nature. This phase marked a shift in Joseph's approach, requiring not just skill but a deep understanding of the human psyche. It was akin to traversing unexplored terrains where each step could unearth a new layer of human complexity, altering his engagement profoundly.

Joseph's quest to restore Marlon's lost memory was a profound expedition into uncharted territories. Every success in uncovering those forgotten fragments didn't just bridge the gap in Marlon's mind but propelled Joseph into a realm where his expertise met unexplored boundaries. With each progress made, Joseph ventured deeper not only into Marlon's psyche but also into the profound depths of his profession. These strides challenged his preconceptions about the capabilities of memory healing, constantly pushing him to reassess the magnitude of his craft.

Each revelation wasn't just a puzzle piece found; it was an expansion of his comprehension, reshaping his understanding of the human mind and the potency of his role as a memory healer.

Joseph found himself amidst a whirlwind of uncertainties stirred by Marlon's request. The quest to reclaim such a profound memory raised a cascade of contemplations within him. He pondered the emotional toll of unearthing a memory tethered to Marlon's tumultuous past. How might this resurfacing affect Marlon's present emotional landscape? Moreover, Joseph grappled with the weighty responsibility that lay ahead. Could he navigate unforeseen consequences arising from this endeavor as a memory healer? The uncertainties swirled around him like a perplexing maze, where every step had the potential to reveal new layers of Marlon's emotions and bring unforeseen impacts to Joseph's professional journey.

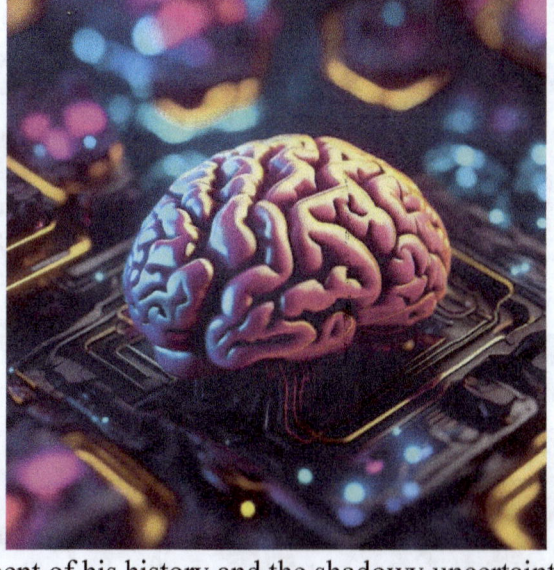

Joseph found himself at a crossroads, caught between Marlon's urgent plea to reclaim a lost fragment of his history and the shadowy uncertainties that loomed ahead.

Marlon's impassioned quest tugged at Joseph's heartstrings, compelling him to embark on a path riddled with unknowns. He recognized this journey as uncharted territory, where each recaptured memory might unfurl a cascade of revelations, some possibly unsettling or disruptive. This expedition resembled navigating a winding road, where every stride might unravel deeper layers of Marlon's intricate past, potentially catalyzing unforeseen shifts within Joseph's own practice and understanding of memory healing. The blend of Marlon's fervor and unforeseen consequences knit together a tapestry of doubts within Joseph's heart.

Joseph's role as a memory gardener became more profound and challenging as he considered guiding Marlon through the labyrinth of his past without disturbing the delicate balance of his present life.

It wasn't solely about retrieving a lost memory fragment; Joseph understood it would be an emotionally charged journey for both Marlon and himself. It meant delicately navigating Marlon's history, shining a light on concealed corners while being wary of how it might impact their present-day existence.

Each progression toward unveiling that memory felt like unwrapping layers of emotions, it was a delicate dance, a journey into emotional depths where uncovering the past could potentially reshape their present lives.

Marlon's plea wasn't merely a task; it was a profound expedition into the depths of someone's thoughts. Joseph faced a demanding challenge, needing not just skill but also ethical consciousness. Delving into Marlon's mind meant unwrapping layers of concealed memories delicately. It wasn't solely about technical expertise—it involved a moral responsibility. Joseph had to respect Marlon's vulnerabilities, handling each memory fragment with the utmost care and sensitivity.

This exploration went beyond unraveling memories; it required honoring the trust placed in him, navigating through emotions, and understanding the impact of each revelation on Marlon's life.

Joseph recognized the imminent journey ahead, one transcending the mere recovery of memories. He braced himself for an expedition with Marlon, foreseeing a profound exploration into uncharted realms. Their quest wasn't solely about memory retrieval; it was a trek through the human psyche, a venture promising both discoveries and potentially challenging repercussions. It involved navigating unfamiliar territories within the human mind, unveiling aspects of Marlon's history shrouded in obscurity. This expedition meant confronting truths concealed within forgotten fragments, poised to unearth a spectrum of the past that awaited illumination.

Joseph faced a pivotal juncture in his career as a memory gardener, teeming with unknowns and uncharted paths.

With each stride, the expedition promised revelations not just about Marlon's past but offered Joseph insights into the intricate tapestry of human existence, enriching both their lives.

Chapter 4

Sowing Memory

Joseph's task was a delicate interplay between nuance and determination as he entered Marlon's world of memories. His method resembled a gardener's careful tending to a fragile flower, balancing precision with unwavering dedication. Each step forward was a deliberate move into Marlon's intricate tapestry of memories, a methodical approach to gently awaken the dormant recollections within Marlon's mind. It required patience and careful attention, much like nurturing the delicate tendrils of a forgotten past, coaxing them back to life. Joseph's journey mirrored the artistry of a gardener, delicately nurturing the faint traces of forgotten memories, fostering their revival.

In the serene embrace of Joseph's home, the day slipped away gently, and Marlon returned, carrying the weight of a forgotten past he sought to illuminate. The intensity in Marlon's eyes spoke volumes, a heaviness hinting at the depth of the untold tale awaiting revelation.

Their meeting marked the threshold of uncharted territory, a realm where forgotten fragments of the past concealed untold secrets. Together, they stood poised to embark on a profound journey, a collaborative exploration set to unravel the intricacies of Marlon's history, and perhaps, unveil transformative truths hidden within those elusive memories.

Joseph's journey into Marlon's mind was akin to a delicate dance, a choreography of patience and precision. He traversed the convoluted pathways where fragments of forgotten memories resided, each one a potential clue to unlocking the deeper recesses of Marlon's thoughts. As he peeled back layers, Joseph didn't just encounter memories; he faced puzzles within complexities nestled within Marlon's consciousness. What started as a task evolved into a captivating exploration, a careful untangling of the intricate threads composing Marlon's obscured past.

Joseph's work embodied the skill of a magician, reviving what time had hidden away. Each memory fragment he brought to light held the promise of becoming a thriving garden of moments.

But this task wasn't just about planting seeds; it was navigating a maze of uncertainties and fragility. With every step into Marlon's past, Joseph carried the responsibility of preserving each memory's truth and purity. It was like safeguarding delicate treasures, shielding them from the chaos of fading remembrances. Joseph's labor wasn't merely about uncovering the past; it was about nurturing and protecting the essence of Marlon's history amidst the complexities of remembrance.

Joseph's journey through Marlon's past was like navigating a complex puzzle, each move revealing a piece of the story. As he delved deeper, the complexities of memory unfolded, challenging Joseph's expertise in piecing together the scattered fragments. The task at hand wasn't just about finding bits of the past; it was about reconstructing a coherent tale distorted by time's passage.

Joseph aimed not only to uncover but also to protect the genuine essence of Marlon's history, ensuring it remained free from any inadvertent alterations or personal biases. This ethical obligation drove his meticulous efforts in weaving an accurate and unblemished narrative from the shards of memory.

Joseph's approach mirrored that of a meticulous artisan crafting a masterpiece. His meticulousness in handling Marlon's memories was akin to a surgeon's precision, delicately maneuvering through each fragment to preserve its authenticity. Every detail he uncovered, whether a gesture, a word, or a memory, held the responsibility of safeguarding the truth of Marlon's history. It was akin to assembling a treasured mosaic, where each piece held significance, contributing to the entirety of Marlon's past. The fragility of these memories demanded careful handling, as any alteration or misplacement could alter the entire narrative, emphasizing the need for Joseph's careful and precise navigation through this intricate tapestry of Marlon's life.

Joseph found himself at a profound crossroads in his work as a memory healer. It wasn't merely about retrieving memories; he realized he was tending to the essence of individuals, nurturing their innermost selves. Each action he took felt like tending to a soul's garden, not just fixing memories but healing the very spirit. The weight of this responsibility resonated deeply within him, transforming his task into a personal journey of understanding human nature at its core. It wasn't solely about recovering a lost memory anymore; it had evolved into an introspective odyssey, exploring the depths of humanity and the significance of our experiences in shaping who we are.

Each memory Joseph found wasn't just a piece of Marlon's past; it was like opening a door to a torrent of feelings and questions, stirring emotions for both of them. It went beyond merely discovering memories; it was about handling the feelings tied to each one.

The real challenge lay not only in reconstructing the past but also in carefully navigating the emotions woven within those memories. It was akin to tiptoeing through a field of emotions, where every step meant delicately managing the sentiments attached to each recollection. It required empathy and finesse to help Marlon process the emotions connected to these memories, creating a safe space amidst the unveiling of the past.

As Joseph and Marlon continued their journey through memories, the boundaries between the past and present began to blur. Every step they took seemed to add new challenges, making their quest for this elusive memory even more intricate. The more they delved, the greater the responsibility felt –

they had to tread cautiously, handling each memory like fragile threads, making sure that their exploration didn't alter the true essence of the past.

The task was to uncover without altering, to navigate through the labyrinth of memories while preserving the authenticity of each thread that wove the story of Marlon's life. Their commitment required a delicate balance between discovery and preservation, honoring the past while navigating the present implications.

Joseph's journey delving into Marlon's past led him beyond the mere act of memory restoration. It became a profound exploration of what it means to be human. With each step, he entered the intricate landscapes of the human mind, witnessing the complexities of emotions and experiences woven into memories.

Chapter 5

Between the
Furrows of the Past

Navigating Marlon's memories posed a substantial challenge for Joseph, pushing the boundaries of his comprehension. It was akin to navigating a complex maze with unpredictable twists and turns. As he delved deeper into Marlon's past, it was like flipping through the pages of a book, each chapter uncovering a web of interconnected memories. Every step into this exploration felt like peeling back another layer of a rich tapestry, unveiling unexpected details that intricately shaped the story. Joseph had to navigate this intricate landscape with care, recognizing that every memory held a piece of Marlon's life puzzle, contributing to a more comprehensive understanding of his experiences and emotions.

In Joseph's day-to-day life, memories flowed in with varying clarity—some vivid, others murky and indistinct. Each memory fragment, whether a clear image or a faint recollection, represented a fraction of a grander narrative.

He carefully sifted through each hint of memory, delving deep into Marlon's past emotions and experiences. It was akin to piecing together a puzzle, where each memory shard, no matter how small or faint, played a crucial role in uncovering the larger, intricate story of Marlon's life. Every emotion and detail held significance in understanding the broader context of Marlon's experiences.

Joseph experienced contrasting emotions that painted his life like a vivid picture book. Sometimes, triumphant moments lit up his days, filling him with pure happiness and the glow of success. Yet, alongside these bright patches were shades of sorrow and traces of loss, echoing the distant past. His life resembled a thrilling rollercoaster ride, a whirlwind of emotions oscillating between exhilarating highs and daunting lows. This mix of feelings sent his heart racing, leaving him caught in an emotional tempest, trying to decipher and navigate through the unpredictable waves of joy, sorrow, and everything in between.

Each moment brought a new color to the canvas of his life, crafting a complex but fascinating mosaic of emotions.

Joseph's journey through Marlon's memories uncovered a treasure trove where even the tiniest moments held profound emotional depth. Each memory shard wasn't just a fact; it was a glimpse into Marlon's deepest thoughts and feelings. These fragments were like puzzle pieces, interlocking to reveal a complex and vivid picture. They showcased how seemingly small incidents had molded Marlon, shaping his present self. Every memory, no matter how fleeting, carried a piece of Marlon's life story.

Yet, in weaving these recollections together, Joseph encountered a common hurdle: distinguishing factual events from the mind's interpretations. The challenge lay in discerning the raw truth from the emotions, biases, or alterations that time and memory could impose on these fragments of the past.

Memories, as time passes, can become fuzzy, a bit unclear about what precisely happened.

They're real, but sometimes colored by personal views or intense emotions, making it hard to tell the absolute truth from how our minds interpret it.

Every tiny detail Joseph found in Marlon's memories was a part of the story Marlon wanted to bring back to life. But it wasn't just about gathering these scattered bits; it was a search for the truth, an attempt to understand what really went down in those distant moments. It involved piecing together a narrative that made sense, staying true to the actual events while preserving the genuine feelings and honesty of each memory.

As Joseph delved deeper into Marlon's memories, it wasn't merely a passive journey through scenes of the past; it became an emotional immersion. He didn't just witness those moments; he felt them deeply, connecting with the emotions and experiences Marlon had lived through.

This went beyond being a bystander; Joseph had to step into the role of an active participant, almost like a storyteller. He needed to understand not just the events but the emotions, the depth of each memory. It was about capturing the essence of those fleeting moments, being able to articulate the significance they held in Marlon's life. Joseph had to absorb and convey the profound impact of those Joseph's role as a memory gardener wasn't just about remembering things—it was about protecting the core of who people were. In this journey through memories, he unearthed the true heart of his job.

It wasn't merely cultivating these memories; it was preserving the essence of those who had been shaped by their experiences. Joseph saw it as a noble mission, going beyond recalling moments. It was about bringing back the purity and truthfulness to each person's life story.

The goal wasn't solely to resurrect faded memories but to ensure that the authenticity and identity of individuals remained intact, untainted by the erosion of time.

Chapter 6

The Roots of the Mystery

Joseph enthusiastically takes on the responsibility of tending to Marlon's memories, fueled by a determination that blends seamlessly with his unquenchable curiosity. With every step deeper into Marlon's memory labyrinth, Joseph discovers an emotional landscape that becomes more intricate with each fragment he unveils. These memories aren't just isolated events on a calendar; they're like threads weaving together an expansive tapestry, displaying the unspoken emotions and complex ties woven into Marlon's life journey. Each memory unraveled isn't merely a moment frozen in time; it's a window into the core of Marlon's experiences, vividly illustrating the vibrant mosaic of a life truly lived. Joseph sees beyond the surface events, understanding that each memory reflects a part of Marlon's soul, each thread a crucial part of the intricate fabric that shapes his existence.

Joseph's journey through Marlon's history is like tending to a garden, where memories are the roots, running deep beneath the surface.

With each exploration, Joseph unearths a mix of emotions—there are moments of regret, instances that puzzle, yet his dedication to unraveling the truth remains steadfast. It's as if he's navigating a maze, every twist and turn revealing new connections, some hidden in shadow but waiting to be discovered and understood. Each memory he unearths isn't just a standalone event; it's a part of a larger network, weaving a story that's rich in emotions and experiences, forming the intricate tapestry of Marlon's life. Joseph continues to delve deeper, knowing that every revealed connection brings him closer to understanding the complex layers of Marlon's past.

These memories, initially disjointed and foggy, gradually intertwine, forming a narrative rich in personal perspectives and emotions.

They're not just recollections of events but windows into Marlon's inner world, painted with his feelings, thoughts, and unique experiences.

As Joseph pieces them together, it's akin to discovering a treasure trove—a collection of moments interwoven with emotions, creating a vivid tapestry that redefines Marlon's life story. This journey reshapes Joseph's understanding, showing him that memories aren't merely factual records but living, emotional imprints that define a person's essence.

Joseph is thrust into a whirlwind of emotions as he navigates through Marlon's memories, a labyrinth teeming with contradictory feelings. It's like sifting through a treasure trove, where each memory shard contains its unique blend of sorrow, regret, hope, and an unyielding pursuit of truth. As Joseph peels through these layers of memories, it's akin to unfurling a grand tapestry, each thread adding depth to Marlon's complex narrative.

The mixture of emotions perplexes Joseph, prompting him to plunge further into the depths of Marlon's recollections.

With every emotional layer unearthed, Joseph finds himself drawn deeper into Marlon's world, attempting to decode the intricate sentiments woven within his memories.

Joseph faces a significant challenge in his task because memories aren't like fixed snapshots; they're more like clay that changes shape over time. Each person's memory is colored by emotions, turning the quest for facts into a complex jigsaw puzzle. Imagine trying to fit puzzle pieces together, but instead of edges. This makes it hard for Joseph to distinguish between the true events and how people recall them due to their emotions. It's like trying to paint a clear picture when the colors keep blending, creating a haze between reality and personal interpretations. This ambiguity makes Joseph's job of stitching together a coherent narrative a tough puzzle to solve.

In his journey through Marlon's memories, Joseph encounters a maze—a complex network of experiences locked away within Marlon's mind.

Each memory uncovered isn't just a snapshot; it's a doorway leading to a cascade of inquiries, tossing Joseph into a vast sea of human emotions, each revelation exposes a fresh layer underneath, each with its mysteries. This process forces Joseph to navigate deeper into the ocean of emotions, challenging his preconceived notions about Marlon's past. It's a continuous reassessment, reshaping the once seemingly clear narrative into a more intricate and nuanced story.

Joseph's path as a memory caretaker transforms into a heartfelt journey for both Marlon and himself.

Picture it as exploring a mysterious cave, every stride uncovering hidden corners, each turn revealing more layers within Marlon's life narrative.

This expedition extends beyond uncovering mere events; it's about grasping the feelings, the concealed depths, and the unseen facets of Marlon's history that add depth to his story.

Every memory holds not just facts but emotions, painting a vivid and detailed portrait of Marlon's experiences, enriching the canvas of his past with intricate and meaningful hues.

Chapter 7

Twilight of the Past

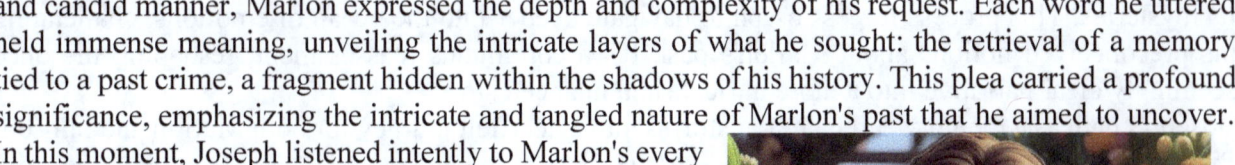

Joseph was absorbed in his work, diving into his tasks with full concentration. His room usually held a quiet peace, with only the sound of his pen scribbling notes filling the air. But this serenity was disrupted by a deliberate knock on his door, breaking the stillness that enveloped his sanctuary. The knock echoed, interrupting his focused state and drawing his attention away from his work. It felt like a sudden interruption, a shift from the calm and solitary ambiance he had been immersed in moments before.

Marlon's arrival at Joseph's peaceful home brought an aura of enigma with him. As he entered Joseph's space, it felt like he carried a trove of untold tales within him. You could sense a lot just by looking at him.

His eyes, weathered by life's ups and downs, seemed to hold many stories that he hadn't shared.

Marlon returned to Joseph's doorstep after a span of days, and there was something noticeably different about him this time. He seemed burdened, carrying a weighty emotional load that was more pronounced than before.

His demeanor shifted, exuding a mix of trust and vulnerability as he opened up to Joseph. In a sincere and candid manner, Marlon expressed the depth and complexity of his request. Each word he uttered held immense meaning, unveiling the intricate layers of what he sought: the retrieval of a memory tied to a past crime, a fragment hidden within the shadows of his history. This plea carried a profound significance, emphasizing the intricate and tangled nature of Marlon's past that he aimed to uncover.

In this moment, Joseph listened intently to Marlon's every word, his cautious nature guiding him to absorb each detail deeply. Marlon's plea wasn't simple; it held a heaviness that made Joseph both curious and wary.

He felt a mix of interest and wariness, understanding that what lay ahead was complex and filled with unknowns. He knew this wasn't an ordinary task—it was a challenge that would bring hurdles and surprises along the way. Joseph prepared himself mentally for this expedition, knowing it would require patience, care, and an open mind. Despite the uncertainty, he readied himself to navigate through uncharted territory, expecting twists, turns, and revelations beyond his anticipation.

He approached his task with meticulous care, akin to an artist shaping a precious creation. He wasn't merely diving into Marlon's memories; he was like an explorer venturing into uncharted territories, searching for lost fragments hidden in the depths of forgotten recollections. Each detail Joseph unearthed was like a treasure, a valuable piece of the puzzle needed to reconstruct Marlon's elusive memory. His approach mirrored the precision of an

archaeologist delicately uncovering ancient artifacts, handling each fragment with deep respect and attention.

With every piece he recovered, Joseph was piecing together a story, handling each detail as a precious gem, understanding its significance in unraveling Marlon's concealed past.

As Joseph ventured deeper into Marlon's history, the gravity of his role began to crystalize. The weight of responsibility settled on his shoulders, a weight that wasn't just about retrieving memories but about honoring the essence of Marlon's life. With each step, Joseph felt a surge of emotions—empathy for Marlon's journey, determination to piece together the fragments, and a deep sense of commitment to give those forgotten memories a voice. It wasn't just a job; it became a heartfelt mission, a vow to breathe life back into the forgotten chapters of Marlon's past. Each step he took was a journey into emotional complexities, discovering a mix of happiness and sadness intricately woven together.

These where moments of triumph collided with moments of despair, forming a roller coaster of feelings. Every memory snippet he revealed was akin to a chapter in a book, holding the significance of events that had a profound impact on Marlon's life. It was as if Joseph was piecing together a narrative, gradually understanding the layers that shaped Marlon's experiences and emotions. As Joseph delved further into Marlon's memories, it was like navigating a maze with interconnected paths. Each memory wasn't isolated but connected to others, forming a complex web that linked moments, people, and feelings in Marlon's mind. But these connections weren't simple; they twisted and turned, revealing the intricate nature of the story. The deeper Joseph went, the more he realized how Marlon's personal viewpoints blurred the line between reality and emotion. This made it challenging to separate factual events from the way Marlon felt about them, adding a new level of complexity to Joseph's mission to unearth the authentic truth behind Marlon's memories.

Delving into Marlon's memories was akin to exploring a vast ocean of feelings and recollections. As Joseph unearthed each memory fragment, it wasn't merely uncovering isolated moments; rather, it was like discovering another layer of a complex, interwoven story. Every detail acted as a new chapter, drawing Joseph deeper into the labyrinth of Marlon's past. It felt like wandering through a maze where emotions and experiences were intertwined, forming a tangled yet captivating tale. With each revelation, Joseph became more immersed in Marlon's emotional landscape, feeling the weight and complexity of intertwined sentiments and past occurrences that shaped Marlon's life. It was a journey that continuously unfolded, offering new insights into Marlon's intricate world.

Joseph's commitment to his mission stood resolute, unwavering in the face of the emotional torrents that accompanied every memory's revelation. Each fragment unearthed seemed like a thread, weaving into Marlon's intricate life story, carrying its emotional weight.

Some recollections echoed with regret, painting scenes tinged with sorrow, while others gleamed with redemption or the fervor of seeking truth. Each memory held a distinct emotional hue, contributing to the rich tapestry of Marlon's past.

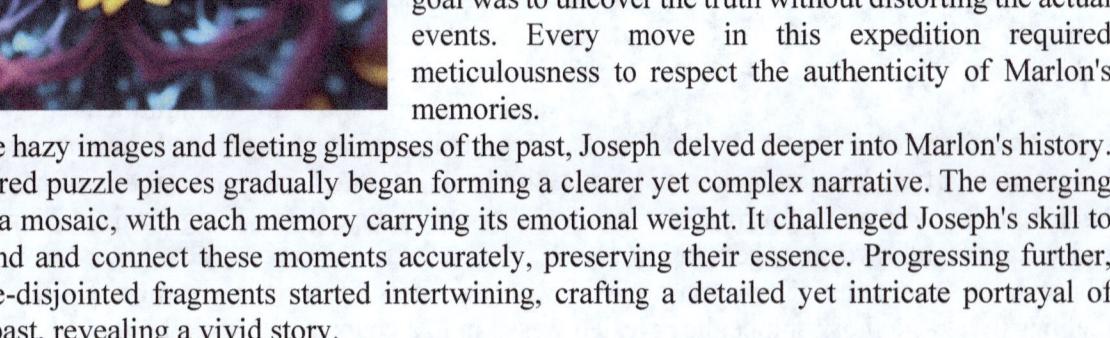

He grappled with a profound challenge. He navigated the fine line between factual occurrences and the subjective lens through which memories had formed in Marlon's mind. Joseph recognized the fragility of these memories, acknowledging the delicate nature of his role. His dedication stemmed from this awareness, knowing the importance of handling these precious fragments with care, preserving their essence, and respecting their emotional significance.

Each step forward was taken with precision and care, akin to navigating through a maze of recollections. His goal was to uncover the truth without distorting the actual events. Every move in this expedition required meticulousness to respect the authenticity of Marlon's memories.

Amidst the hazy images and fleeting glimpses of the past, Joseph delved deeper into Marlon's history. The scattered puzzle pieces gradually began forming a clearer yet complex narrative. The emerging story was a mosaic, with each memory carrying its emotional weight. It challenged Joseph's skill to comprehend and connect these moments accurately, preserving their essence. Progressing further, these once-disjointed fragments started intertwining, crafting a detailed yet intricate portrayal of Marlon's past, revealing a vivid story.

Joseph approached each memory fragment with utmost care, recognizing their profound significance. The weight of these memories, laden with emotions, became palpable as he navigated through them. His dedication to reconstructing these fragments with sensitivity was evident, realizing the impact they might have on Marlon's well-being. Amidst this determination, a sense of concern burgeoned within Joseph regarding how these revelations might affect Marlon emotionally.

Josephde termined to decode its secrets while treading cautiously, aware of the potential impact on Marlon's present emotional landscape.

Chapter 8

Flowers of Truth

Joseph found himself immersed in Marlon's memories, each passing day feeling like a venture into an entirely new world, one woven from these fragments of the past. It was as if he had stepped beyond the boundaries of the ordinary and into a realm crafted from these intricately intertwined memories. Over time, these fragments began to coalesce, painting a comprehensive and vivid image, a story that was both complex and deeply touching.

With every unveiled detail, it felt like a portal opening into a chamber of emotions. These memories transcended mere accounts of the crime; they were more like pieces of a larger mosaic, illustrating the intricate web of human connections. Initially disparate scenes began to interlock, revealing ties that had long remained concealed.

Each memory, once isolated, now became a thread in a larger narrative, unveiling hidden layers of emotions, unearthing relationships, and exposing the intricate tapestry of sentiments woven through time.

For Joseph, this task was akin to delving into the essence of human experience, far more than a mere gathering of facts. It felt like unwrapping the layers of the human heart, where each memory wasn't just a recollection but a repository of emotions. Entering this realm was like stepping into a living painting, where each memory wasn't just an event but a vibrant expression of feelings. These memories were like windows into intricate emotional landscapes, each carrying its own weight of honesty and depth. They weren't just scenes but entire worlds teeming with sentiments. Every uncovered memory acted as a stroke on the canvas, painting a vivid and emotionally rich portrayal of Marlon's past, adding layers of depth and intricacy to the overall narrative.

Joseph's journey through Marlon's memories was a constant revelation. With every new detail, his understanding evolved, reshaping the narrative he initially perceived. It wasn't solely about the sequence of events; rather, it unfolded into a complex web of connections.

Each twist and turn in the story revealed a deeper layer, not just about the crime itself but the emotions entwined within it. Beyond the actions laid bare, Joseph unearthed the inner struggles, fears, and conflicts of the individuals involved. It wasn't merely a recounting of events; it was a vivid portrayal of how these moments were shaped by the intricate tapestry of human emotions, painting a more profound picture of Marlon's past.

His exploration into Marlon's past wasn't just uncovering facts; it was like discovering hidden treasures within relationships. With every new detail, the story expanded beyond the mere events. It became a vivid display of the connections between people, weaving a tapestry of human bonds.

It wasn't merely about deciphering a crime but delving into the dance of emotions and interactions. Each revealed detail was like a note in a symphony, painting a broader and more colorful picture of the relationships that existed beneath the surface.

His quest was akin to peering beyond the actions, uncovering the pulsating rhythm of connections that formed the heart of Marlon's history.

Joseph's journey through Marlon's memories wasn't just about unearthing facts; it was a rollercoaster of emotions. With every new detail revealed, a wave of pressure crashed over him, like a weight pressing down on his shoulders. Each revelation wasn't just information; it was a surge of feelings, a mix of curiosity tangled with the emotional weight of uncovering the past. He found himself walking a tightrope between his hunger for truth and the immense emotional impact each discovery carried.

It was like trying to maintain equilibrium while navigating a storm of conflicting emotions, where the weight of the discoveries bore down heavily, testing his ability to remain steadfast in his quest for truth despite the overwhelming emotional toll.

Joseph's journey through Marlon's memories was an emotional odyssey, one that drew him closer to the heart of Marlon's experiences.

Every memory revealed wasn't just a story; it was a reflection of emotions Joseph could empathize with deeply. Each piece of Marlon's past unearthed a part of Joseph's own feelings—echoes of hurt, struggles, and a yearning for clarity that resonated within him. These memories seemed like long-forgotten whispers, yearning to break free from the shadows. They carried narratives woven with pain, uncertainty, and an underlying desire for understanding and closure. As Joseph delved deeper into Marlon's past, it felt as if he was deciphering the roadmap to Marlon's soul, forging a stronger connection through shared emotions and experiences.

Every step he took wasn't solely about uncovering the facts; it was an attempt to comprehend the intricate tapestry of feelings that colored those bygone moments. The memories weren't just about events but about the emotions intertwined within them, shaping Marlon's experiences and adding layers of depth to Joseph's exploration.

Chapter 9

The Shadow
of Conflict

Joseph's journey through Marlon's memories was like navigating a labyrinth of emotions, each turn revealing a new layer of complexity. It felt as though he was piecing together a vast puzzle, where each revelation added depth to the story. However, with each detail came a surge of emotions, almost like adding weight to an already heavy burden. Joseph wasn't merely uncovering events; he was experiencing the emotions woven into each memory. The more he unraveled, the greater the emotional load became, as he realized the significance and impact these memories carried. It was a delicate balance between unveiling the past and shouldering the weight of its profound emotional resonance.

Joseph found himself in an emotional conflict, torn between his commitment to Marlon and the apprehension about the repercussions of unraveling these memories.

His dedication to Marlon's cause was unwavering, feeling duty-bound to piece together every hidden fragment, bringing clarity to the shadows of the past.

However, this dedication came with a twinge of unease, a discomfort about the potential impact these memories might have on others tied to the story. While he remained fiercely loyal to Marlon, a part of him was concerned about the wider ramifications, uncertain about the unforeseen consequences these revelations might trigger for everyone involved in the intricate web of memories.

Joseph remained resolute in his quest to unearth Marlon's forgotten memories, recognizing the weight of emotions each piece carried. As he delved deeper, every fragment uncovered seemed to add another layer to the tale, a rich tapestry woven with intricate details and profound connections. It was akin to navigating through a labyrinth, with each twist and turn unveiling a new facet of the story, illuminating the complex interweaving of relationships that enveloped those significant moments.

Each disclosure drew Joseph further into this convoluted network of memories, his determination to piece together the mosaic of Marlon's past growing stronger. Marlon's emotions were vividly present in his every movement and uttered word, adding depth and intensity to the journey Joseph undertook, providing crucial cues to the hidden corners of his memories and feelings. Marlon's eyes reflected a complex medley of emotions that Joseph couldn't ignore. Within their depths, there was an unmistakable blend of pain and concern,

intermingled with a faint trace of hope and uneasiness. It felt as though Marlon's entire existence encapsulated the inner battle and tension associated with resurrecting those deeply buried memories. His soft spoken words, laden with a profound weight, seemed to carry stories of historical torment and a deep yearning to rediscover what had faded into the recesses of time. His expressions conveyed a struggle between the desire to remember and the fear of what those memories might unveil, portraying a poignant narrative of emotional turmoil and an earnest quest for forgotten truths.

Joseph found himself entangled in a web of conflicting concerns. On one side, his dedication to Marlon's well-being urged him to dig deep into these memories, to unearth every fragment for Marlon's sake. Yet, on the other side, loomed the worry of the fallout—the ripple effect that these unveiled memories might have on everyone linked to Marlon's past. He was at a crossroads, torn between the responsibility to reveal the truth and the fear of causing unintended pain. Balancing Marlon's needs with the potential impact on others became an emotional struggle, a tug-of-war between honoring Marlon's history and protecting the emotions of those connected to him. This inner conflict weighed heavily on Joseph, dictating a careful, measured approach in navigating this delicate terrain of forgotten recollections.

Joseph encountered a challenging dilemma, caught between two important responsibilities. On one side, his dedication to resurrect Marlon's forgotten memories tugged at him, urging him to uncover each fragment.

However, this commitment clashed with his profound worry about the wider repercussions on those connected to these memories. Each move to reveal the truth felt like navigating a battlefield within himself. On one front stood his allegiance to Marlon, pushing him to unravel every piece. On the other, the concern about potential harm to others involved in Marlon's past presented a formidable obstacle. This internal conflict weighed heavily on Joseph, torn between honoring his duty to Marlon and the ethical dilemma of potentially affecting others beyond their immediate sphere. Joseph encountered a persistent inner struggle, torn between his unwavering loyalty to Marlon and the broader implications of his role as a memory caretaker. This ongoing conflict stirred a whirlwind of conflicting emotions within him, forcing him into a profound contemplation about the depth and scope of his work, his dedication to Marlon urged him to uncover every memory, fulfilling his commitment to his client.

However, this dedication clashed with the wider implications of his role, prompting a deep state of reflection about the significance of his responsibilities as a memory cultivator. It made him question the impact of his actions beyond Marlon's immediate sphere and pondered the ethical dimensions of his role in reviving memories while considering their potential effects on others.

Chapter 10

The Breaking Point

Joseph's task started with a clear direction but soon took an unexpected turn, leaving him adrift in a sea of perplexity and emotions. The story he worked diligently to reconstruct suddenly became a tangled web due to a surprising twist in Marlon's recollection. It felt like the solid ground he stood on crumbled beneath him, shaking the foundation of his efforts. Each new detail he uncovered seemed to add confusion rather than clarity, resembling pieces of a puzzle that refused to fit together as anticipated. This unforeseen development disrupted the flow of his work, throwing him into a realm of uncertainty and making the process of reconstructing Marlon's memories challenging and uncertain. Joseph's tranquil exploration of Marlon's past took an unexpected turn when a surprising revelation disrupted the clarity he thought he had. It felt like a sudden gust of wind disturbing the carefully arranged memories, creating a whirlwind of uncertainty.

The solid foundation of his understanding seemed shaken, leaving Joseph feeling disoriented and doubtful about the truths he had previously perceived. What once appeared crystal clear now seemed hazy, as if the ground beneath his comprehension of Marlon's narrative had been unsettled. This unexpected twist left Joseph feeling unsure, prompting him to reevaluate the entirety of Marlon's story, recognizing that the reality might not be as straightforward as he had initially thought.

Joseph's orderly understanding of Marlon's narrative took a sharp turn as unexpected details surfaced, contradicting his preconceptions. These revelations shattered the coherent story Joseph had meticulously constructed, causing it to crumble into uncertainty. It was like watching the pieces of a puzzle scatter without fitting together as they once did. This abrupt shift disrupted Joseph's confidence, igniting a series of perplexing questions. The newfound information not only challenged the truthfulness of his previously woven storyline but also shook his confidence in his role within this intricate tale.

It left him grappling with doubts about his perception, the reliability of the story, and his place in deciphering Marlon's enigmatic past.

Joseph found himself caught in a storm of uncertainty, standing at a crossroads of critical decisions. The emergence of unexpected facts felt like a sudden whirlwind, pulling him into uncharted territories where every step carried an unpredictable outcome. Amid this turbulence, he faced a pivotal choice:

continue forging ahead despite the shattering of his established beliefs or halt to reevaluate the entire foundation he had meticulously built.

The confusion that enveloped Joseph was akin to being lost in a labyrinth of choices, each carrying its own weighty implications. It was a moment of profound contemplation, where Joseph grappled with the uncertainty of forging ahead into the unknown or taking a pause to recalibrate his understanding.

Joseph found himself in a perplexing situation, torn between moving forward into uncertainty or retracing his steps to reevaluate his chosen path. This sudden shift in the narrative stirred up a storm of conflicting emotions within him. It shattered his confidence in reconstructing the story as he had envisioned. Each decision he pondered involved reshaping his entire perception of past events, yet it came with risks. The consequences of his actions might ripple far beyond Marlon's story, impacting others intricately entwined in these memories. It became a delicate balancing act between reshaping the narrative and understanding the potential repercussions it could hold for everyone involved. Joseph grappled with the weight of each step, aware of the wider implications of his choices. Joseph suddenly found himself inundated by a flood of emotions, each one carrying a tremendous weight that felt almost unbearable. This surge of feelings came crashing down upon him, making it challenging to navigate the path forward.

The choices he faced seemed monumental, and the revelation of this new reality disrupted his entire understanding of the situation. It was as if he was in a battle within himself, torn between conflicting emotions and the need to make pivotal decisions in the midst of this upheaval. The intensity of this emotional turmoil left him grappling with a sense of internal conflict, making each decision a daunting challenge. Joseph found himself enveloped in a cloud of uncertainty that lingered persistently, not only questioning his ability to grasp the intricacies of the past but also his role within Marlon's narrative. This doubt seemed to shadow his every step, creating a sense of unease and instability. It was akin to traversing on an unstable surface, where each direction held an equal chance of leading to further ambiguity. He grappled with a feeling of being adrift, unsure of how to proceed within the complex framework of Marlon's memories.

The uncertainty surrounding his understanding of the past and his place in unraveling these memories left him feeling disoriented, hesitant, and cautious about his next move.

Joseph found himself in a delicate position, juggling the weight of his loyalty to Marlon with the apprehension of the potential repercussions that might stem from his quest to uncover buried memories. The mounting emotional strain pressed upon him, resembling a steadily growing burden. Each step forward felt uncertain, as if navigating a precarious path where the consequences remained uncertain. It was a persistent internal struggle, a balancing act between his commitment to support Marlon and the apprehension about the repercussions

that might unfold as a result of unveiling buried truths. Joseph feared that his actions, while aimed at aiding Marlon, could potentially disrupt the lives of everyone intertwined within this intricate web of forgotten recollections, causing an unforeseen upheaval that could affect them profoundly.

This conflict of obligations created a constant state of tension and uncertainty for Joseph as he treaded carefully through uncharted emotional territory.

Joseph reached a pivotal moment where his feelings and doubts clashed fiercely. With every fresh detail, the narrative he had painstakingly crafted seemed to crumble like a house of cards, throwing him into an internal conflict that felt like a battlefield. He had stitched together a version of Marlon's story from the fragments of memories he'd collected, but now, these new revelations rocked the very foundation of that constructed tale. It was as if the ground beneath him was shifting, leaving him grappling with a whirlwind of doubt and conflicting emotions that challenged the reality he thought he knew.

Each piece of information acted like a bomb, exploding the carefully woven threads of the story and leaving him stranded amidst the rubble of uncertainty.

Joseph grappled not only with the task of rebuilding these memories but also with the ethical responsibility of how his decisions might echo through the lives intertwined within this intricate web of recollections.

Chapter 11

The Labyrinth
of Memories

Joseph embarks on an intensive journey, fervently determined to navigate the labyrinth of Marlon's memories. At the outset, these recollections appear fragmented, dispersed across time and space. Yet, with every step forward, each memory strand interlaces with another, forming an intricate fabric of Marlon's past. The task transcends mere proficiency as a memory caretaker; it demands a profound grasp of the interwoven threads within Marlon's mind. Imagine assembling a puzzle where the pieces not only fit in a physical sense but also convey emotions and nuances. Joseph's pursuit isn't solely about skill; it requires an intuitive understanding, an ability to see beyond the surface and discern the underlying connections that bind these memories together, painting a comprehensive picture of Marlon's history.

Joseph finds himself confronted with unforeseen twists and revelations, reshaping the story's landscape into a labyrinth of intricate details beyond his initial expectations.

Each turn unearths layers previously obscured, reframing the narrative in unexpected ways. It's as if he's delving into a vivid tapestry woven not just with events but also with the emotions and perspectives surrounding them. This process feels akin to solving a puzzle where the pieces don't align as anticipated; instead, they divulge a more elaborate and nuanced picture. The memories aren't merely factual occurrences but an amalgamation of subjective experiences and objective realities, intertwining to create a narrative that surpasses initial assumptions, revealing a multi-faceted and profound story.

Joseph is caught in a challenging mission, striving to weave together these fragmented memories into a coherent and truthful tale. The difficulty arises from a clash between two versions of reality: the emotions people experienced in the past versus their present recollections.

This clash adds layers of complexity to the task, demanding a sharp ability to discern between personal perceptions and the factual occurrences. It's akin to unraveling the differences between immediate impressions and how those impressions have evolved over time. This struggle deepens the narrative, complicating the process of reconstructing events as they truly unfolded from the tangled web of memories shaped by both emotions and the passage of time.

In this convoluted journey through memories, each revelation seems tinged with the emotions and perspectives of those involved. The narrative isn't just about events; it's a canvas painted with the feelings and unique views of each participant. Joseph finds himself engulfed in a whirlpool of conflicting emotions, torn between the imperative to accurately reconstruct the past and the intricate emotions interlaced in every memory. It's akin to sailing through an ocean of emotions that ripple through each fragment of the story, blurring the line between objective reality and the personal experiences embedded within.

This intricate interplay challenges Joseph's understanding, demanding a delicate balance between uncovering factual events and acknowledging the human sentiments woven into each memory. Navigating Marlon's memories takes Joseph into uncharted territories of complexity. The challenge transforms, not just about recalling the events, but understanding the tangled web of interpretations woven around each memory. It's akin to untangling a knotted rope: each twist holds layers of meaning. Joseph faces a task demanding not only technical prowess but also emotional acumen. It's not merely sorting through memories; it's deciphering emotions, nuances, and different viewpoints embedded within each recollection. To unravel the genuine truth amidst these complexities requires not just knowledge but empathy, intuition, and a deep understanding of human emotions and perspectives. It's an intricate puzzle where the layers must be peeled back delicately, revealing the core truth hidden within each memory.

Every turn presents a choice: to reveal a new path or plunge into another enigmatic twist, amplifying the challenge and casting uncertainty on Joseph's path forward. The task demands patience, skill, and adaptability as he maneuvers through this intricate landscape of recollections.

Chapter 12

The Fragility
of Truth

Joseph faces a colossal task as he navigates through Marlon's intricate web of memories. This challenge surpasses mere reconstruction; it's an endeavor that delves deeper than stringing together events of the past. It's like stepping into a maze where every turn uncovers not just incidents but emotions, perceptions, and the complexities of human experience. The challenge lies not only in piecing together what happened but in deciphering the emotional layers, the hidden feelings attached to each memory. It demands more than just stitching events—it requires understanding the profound impact of those experiences on Marlon's life and how they interlace with his emotions, forming a complex tapestry that shapes his world. Joseph's journey through Marlon's memories turned into an emotional rollercoaster, each new detail stirring up a tempest within him. It's like his own emotions were entangled with the threads of Marlon's story, woven into its very essence.

With every turn in Marlon's recollections, Joseph faced an inner battle. The challenge was grappling with how to stay devoted to these emerging memories while staying true to his own sense of what felt truthful and right. It felt like treading a precarious path, trying to uphold the integrity of the newly surfaced truths while remaining faithful to his instincts about what seemed authentic and genuine in Marlon's complex tapestry of memories.

Joseph's journey into Marlon's memories became a tumultuous river of doubts and conflicting emotions. The deeper he ventured, the more his personal feelings collided with the duty he bore as a memory keeper. Each unveiled memory seemed like a thread woven into the fabric of truth, but instead of clarifying, it added layers of complexity.

Each new detail felt like a double-edged sword, offering insights but also casting shadows of doubt on the solidity of the narrative he struggled to reconstruct. The journey became a battle between the pursuit of truth and the muddled uncertainties embedded within Marlon's memories. Joseph's commitment to seeking truth amid the swirling emotions and tangled memories posed a profound

challenge: what did truth truly represent in this complex labyrinth of recollections? Each fragment of memory reflected not only Marlon's past but also Joseph's own uncertainties and doubts. As a memory gardener, his struggle was apparent—the personal lens through which he viewed these memories clouded the quest for an objective reality. Every unveiled detail felt like a puzzle piece, blurring the line between actual events and the subjective interpretations woven into the narrative. Rather than untangling, the story's intricacy grew, creating a web of uncertainties and complexities that challenged the very foundation of understanding the past.

The truth he sought seemed elusive amidst the interplay of memories and personal perspectives. Joseph's internal struggle intensified within the intricate network of memories he traversed. The challenge loomed large: how to harmonize his own emotions and viewpoints with the imperative to maintain the authenticity of the unfolding narrative? It felt akin to merging his personal perceptions and feelings with the duty of accurately depicting the historical sequence of events. In essence, he grappled with aligning his inner beliefs, experiences, and biases with the larger responsibility of presenting an unbiased and faithful portrayal of the past. It's a delicate balancing act, where his own emotions and perspectives walk hand in hand with the commitment to unearth the genuine truths concealed within Marlon's memories. Within the intricate web of memories, Joseph encountered a tumultuous storm of emotions that disrupted his path.

The lines between raw factual occurrences and subjective interpretations blurred, entangling him in a perplexing dilemma. As he delved deeper, a fog of uncertainty enveloped his journey.

Each step felt like navigating through a maze where the distinction between objective reality and subjective perception became increasingly ambiguous. This amalgamation of emotions and events caused a whirlwind within him, casting doubt on the solidity of his discoveries and challenging the very foundation of his understanding. It was a turbulent struggle, where his personal feelings clashed with the fidelity of the narrative he sought to unveil, making the quest for truth an intricate battle within himself.

In navigating the intricate labyrinth of memories, Joseph faced a daunting challenge: distinguishing objective truth from his own subjective viewpoint. Each stride deeper into this intricate maze amplified his struggle with the fragility of facts and his susceptibility to emotions.

It felt akin to treading through an ocean of uncertainties, where every revelation submerged him further into a pool of ambiguity. The past events intertwined with his personal interpretation, clouding the distinction between what genuinely occurred and how he perceived it.

This inner conflict was like trying to separate grains of sand from water—it seemed almost impossible to

discern the unaltered truth from the ripples of his own biases and feelings within this complex tapestry of memories.

Joseph found himself entangled in a story that seemed like a jigsaw puzzle missing some crucial pieces. As he reconstructed the tale, aiming for authenticity, he confronted a formidable challenge. The facts, the real events, clashed with his emotions and perspectives, creating friction in weaving an accurate narrative. It felt like a constant battle, torn between the obligation to uphold the truth and the influence of his own sentiments on shaping the story.

He aimed to portray an objective picture, but the emotional tides within him threatened to distort the very fabric of the narrative, complicating the process of stitching together an authentic depiction of events. Joseph finds himself navigating a turbulent journey where the line between facts and feelings blurs into a storm of emotions.

As he delves deeper into the complexities of memories, the solidity of truth seems fragile, almost wavering amid uncertainties. The quest for authenticity isn't just about piecing together events anymore. It's an intricate puzzle of sorting through conflicting perspectives, where the objective truth intertwines with personal perceptions. This emotional tempest challenges Joseph, as the journey shifts from uncovering past occurrences to understanding the intricate web of human experiences and the subtle nuances that shape our understanding of what is real and what is perceived.

Chapter 13

In the Light of the Past

Joseph finds himself engulfed in a whirlwind of unexpected discoveries as he sifts through Marlon's memories. Each new fragment he unearths feels like a surprise, offering glimpses into a reality he hadn't foreseen. These scattered bits of memory, as he gathers them, begin to interlock, revealing a broader narrative that not only depicts Marlon's past but also triggers profound reflections within Joseph. With every deeper dive into these recollections, they disclose layers of intricacy, weaving a more intricate fabric of moments that unravel more than just Marlon's history—it unravels Joseph's inner contemplations too. As the past unfolds, it serves not only as a window into Marlon's world but also as a mirror reflecting Joseph's own thoughts and musings. Joseph's recent discoveries have halted him in his tracks, sparking profound contemplation. Every fresh detail acts as a spotlight, illuminating past events and prompting him to ponder the intricacies of human nature.

It feels akin to unraveling the layers of a complex puzzle, exposing how our histories influence and mold us, often in ways that go unnoticed. These revelations have prompted Joseph to delve deeper into the workings of the human mind and the connections between our experiences and the people we become. The process is akin to peering into a mirror reflecting the shaping force of our past on our present selves. Memories are like hidden wizards in Joseph's eyes. They're not just tales of the past; they wield a mighty force, sculpting how people perceive the world and even guide their future actions. It's almost like these memories possess their own enchantment, a magical spell that shapes individuals' thoughts and influences their choices. Joseph is struck by the incredible influence these memories hold over someone's life, how they serve as guides, shaping decisions, and forming the lenses through which people view their world.

It's astonishing to him how these seemingly intangible fragments from the past can weave a profound impact on present actions and future pathways.

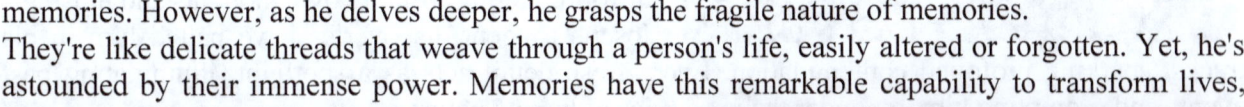

Joseph's mind gets a jolt as he contemplates the profound nature of memory. It's not just about recalling events; it's a force that molds our identities. He's struck by the idea that memories aren't just stagnant pictures of the past; they're active players shaping our present and future. It amazes him how these recollections don't merely recount tales; they actively influence our choices and actions ahead. Memories, are these potent instruments that sculpt our paths, dictating who we evolve into. It's intriguing for Joseph to grasp that these seemingly intangible recollections possess the power to steer the course of someone's life, acting as architects of future endeavors and defining one's essence. He ponders the profound impact of life experiences on shaping individual identities.

He sees these experiences as the building blocks that construct our personalities and perspectives. Memories, in his contemplation, are captivating because they don't just recall events; they have the remarkable ability to evoke emotions and alter our comprehension of situations. It's intriguing to him how memories serve as a dual force—they possess the potential to facilitate healing by revisiting positive experiences, yet simultaneously, they can also incite turmoil and disagreements when recollections of past conflicts resurface. He finds it fascinating how these recollections can be both a source of solace and a catalyst for unrest, showcasing the multifaceted nature of memory's influence on our lives.

Joseph's journey into Marlon's memories becomes a profound experience, triggering a deeper understanding of the significance of his role. Initially, he views his task as simply restoring forgotten memories. However, as he delves deeper, he grasps the fragile nature of memories.

They're like delicate threads that weave through a person's life, easily altered or forgotten. Yet, he's astounded by their immense power. Memories have this remarkable capability to transform lives, influencing how individuals perceive themselves and the world around them. Joseph begins to appreciate the immense impact his work holds, not just in retrieving lost recollections but in realizing the transformative potential of memories in shaping and reshaping one's life story. He recognizes that memories aren't just fragments of the past but pivotal forces shaping present and future narratives. Joseph's journey goes beyond mere memory reconstruction; it's a vast exploration into the intricacies of human existence. As he unravels memories, he's diving into profound questions about the essence of humanity itself. He's intrigued by the intricate relationship between memory and identity, contemplating how our past experiences intertwine with our core being.

There's this curiosity about how memories sculpt the very essence of who we are, sculpting our beliefs, emotions, and actions. He's reflecting on the profound impact memories hold, recognizing how our interpretations of the past significantly influence our decisions and choices for the future. Essentially, Joseph is exploring the fundamental connection between memory, identity, and the human experience, aiming to understand how our past shapes our present and molds our future.

Joseph's exploration isn't merely uncovering Marlon's history; it's becoming a reflective experience for him. He's contemplating the complexities of the human mind and the intricate ways it operates.

This journey isn't just about the past; it's an excavation of the human experience itself. He's delving into the connections between our past experiences, our current reality, and the potential future. It's like peering into the interconnected threads of time that weave together to shape who we are.

Joseph's quest is to unravel this intertwined tapestry, understanding how our histories echo through our present moments and even sway the paths we'll tread ahead. He's on a profound exploration of the human psyche, seeking to comprehend the intricate interplay between memory, the present, and the future in defining our existence.

Joseph's journey through Marlon's memories isn't just unraveling a narrative; it's unraveling him too. He's at this crossroads, trying to strike a balance between two worlds. One side is his role as a meticulous architect, reconstructing Marlon's story, carefully assembling each fragment into a coherent whole. Yet, there's this personal pull, an inquisitiveness ignited by the unexpected twists and turns within these memories. As he progresses, the challenge intensifies; reconciling his commitment to Marlon with his sheer fascination becomes a daily struggle. It's akin to walking a tightrope, aiming to maintain an equilibrium where neither duty nor intrigue outweighs the other.

The delicate act of balancing these two facets feels like tending to two fragile scales, where a single miscalculation could tip the entire narrative into disarray.

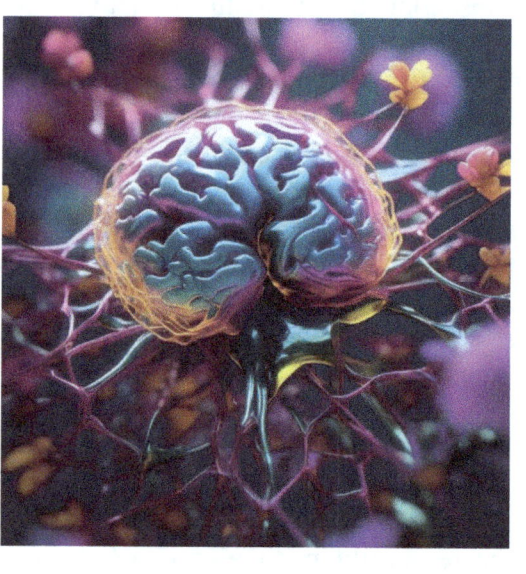

Chapter 14

The Reflection of Decision

Joseph stands at a crucial moment, emotions swirling within like a storm. The intensity of feelings—eagerness, worry, and uncertainty—floods his senses. It's as if he's shrouded in a thick mist, obscuring the right direction to proceed. Marlon's memories, like an intricate maze, sprawl before him. Every pathway seems weighty, laden with consequences. Each decision tugs him in multiple directions, each one leading to outcomes that appear equally challenging. It's a moment of profound dilemma where the choices he makes could define the course of unraveling Marlon's story, and the weight of those decisions feels almost overwhelming. Joseph faces a monumental challenge that burdens him deeply. Each aspect he contemplates feels heavier, adding to the weight on his shoulders. He's grappling with a critical decision: to persist in uncovering the truth despite potential repercussions, or to halt and deliberate, risking the loss of a chance to clarify the situation.

It's akin to a storm raging within him, torn between the responsibility to reveal reality and the prudence of avoiding unintended consequences. The choice feels immense, as though it carries the power to either shed light on the truth or potentially stir up unforeseen difficulties for those involved. The weight of this decision looms large, making every step forward or backward an arduous consideration.

Joseph's journey into Marlon's memories felt like embarking on an epic quest, an uncharted adventure with destinies waiting to unfold. Each decision he faced resembled a fork in the road, a crucial point influencing the direction of the story he was unraveling. He found himself standing at a crossroads, pondering which path to take among numerous potential routes. The gravity of his choices weighed heavily on him, as each direction held the promise of revealing different facets of Marlon's narrative.

Should he delve deeper into certain memories, or pivot towards unexplored avenues? The weight of these decisions amplified the significance of his quest, each choice holding the potential to shape the entire trajectory of Marlon's story.

Joseph found himself caught between two powerful forces, each pulling him in a different direction. One side urged him forward, fueled by an unyielding determination to unearth the truth. This drive within him was relentless, pushing him to persist despite the hurdles, aiming for a complete and comprehensive understanding. He craved resolution, hoping that each uncovered memory would contribute to painting a clearer picture of the past. However, alongside this determination, a sense of apprehension crept in. He grappled with concerns about the potential fallout from his pursuit.

On the other side, the need for a pause, a moment of respite amidst the chaos, tugged at Joseph. Amidst the whirlwind of revelations and the urgency to discover more, there lingered a longing for a brief hiatus. It was as if taking a step back to reflect might provide some clarity amidst the complexity. This internal conflict between advancing relentlessly and pausing to consider the implications was like a tug-of-war between determination and the wisdom of taking a breath amid the storm.

He took a pause, carefully contemplating the weight of each decision and its ripple effect on everyone involved. It was a moment of introspection, where he questioned if his cautious approach might inadvertently hinder uncovering the complete truth. There was this internal debate about whether his careful consideration was inadvertently preventing the revelation of painful yet necessary truths.

He pondered if, in prioritizing the comfort of those entangled in the memories, he might be missing out on crucial pieces that could bring closure and understanding to the entire situation, even if it involved facing difficult realities.

The multitude of choices seemed overwhelming, shrouded in ambiguity. It was akin to navigating uncharted territory, where every direction was obscured by darkness and uncertainty, leaving him feeling like an intrepid explorer searching for a guiding light. Amid this labyrinth of choices, Marlon's reminders echoed in his mind, emphasizing the gravity of his role and the delicate nature of the memories he handled. The decision looming ahead felt colossal, bearing down on his thoughts with immense pressure, each potential outcome carrying its own weighty significance, making the choice an arduous burden on his mind.

The weight of responsibility tugged at him, making each decision feel like a balancing act between uncertainty and the gravity of doing what's morally right. He grappled with a profound dilemma: continue the pursuit of truth, risking potential complications, or pause to contemplate the potential ramifications of his investigation. The dilemma wasn't solely about uncovering facts but considering the ripple effects on numerous lives connected to this intricate web of memories. Should he persist, knowing the revelations might stir trouble, or step back to evaluate the repercussions before proceeding? The moral quandary pressed heavily on him, demanding careful consideration of the paths ahead.

Joseph found himself in the grip of an inner struggle that refused to settle, much like an unrelenting storm churning within him, stirring an endless array of questions and doubts.

Every option he considered felt like a gateway to an entirely different reality, carrying along with it enormous, unknown consequences. Despite yearning for a straightforward, uncomplicated path ahead, this crossroads seemed to ensnare him further in a web of perplexity and ambiguity. The decision looming before Joseph wasn't solely tied to his role as a memory gardener, entwined with unraveling Marlon's past. It stretched beyond, resonating with broader implications and ramifications that could ripple through numerous lives. This wasn't merely about choosing a direction in his investigation; it involved the delicate balance between uncovering truths and safeguarding against unforeseen complexities that might arise from those revelations. Each potential path weighed heavy on his shoulders, laden with uncertainties that refrained from offering a clear way out.

The decisions Joseph was grappling with seemed like a fork in the road, where whichever path he chose could steer the lives of all tied to those memories in a different direction.

Each choice felt weighty, carrying the potential to pivot the course of numerous lives connected to the past he was unraveling. It wasn't merely a decision for him; it was a crucial juncture that merged his responsibility with thoughtful consideration. It was as if he stood at a crossroads, where the direction he picked would ripple through the lives of those involved, influencing their futures based on the choices he made in the present. Every move he contemplated carried the gravity of shaping multiple destinies.

Chapter 15

The Paths
of Memory

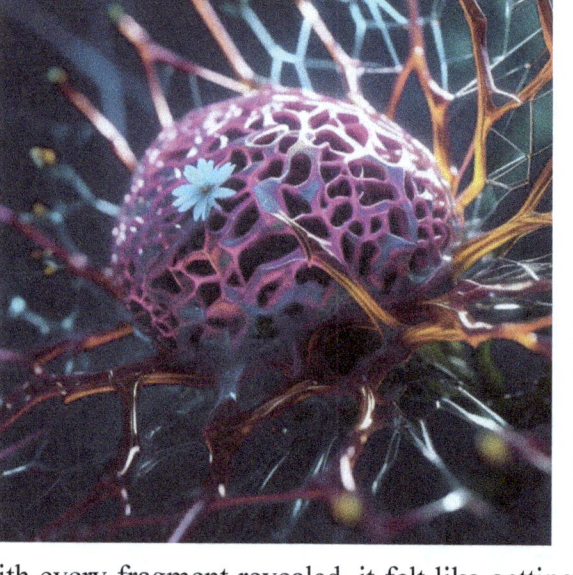

It was emotionally challenging for him, standing at this juncture akin to peeling back the layers of an intricate tale. Imagine it like unwrapping a story, where each revelation wasn't just an answer but a new question that prodded at the very essence of what Joseph believed.

It felt like unraveling a thread that led to a cascade of mysteries, shaking the foundation of his understanding.

Each layer unearthed complexities, painting a picture vastly different from what he initially perceived, making him reevaluate the core of the narrative and challenging his understanding of the entire journey through Marlon's memories.

He seemed to make progress in assembling the memories, fitting each piece together like a complex puzzle.

With every fragment revealed, it felt like getting nearer to the full story, a real achievement in this quest for truth. But surprisingly, as the picture became clearer, it brought unforeseen challenges. The responsibility of managing these memories began to feel heavy, like carrying a massive weight on his shoulders. Each discovery stirred up a whirlwind of emotions within Joseph. Alongside that emotional whirlwind, questions started surfacing, challenging his initial expectations and leading to uncertainties he hadn't anticipated. It was as if the clarity he sought came with a trade-off, introducing a whole new set of complexities and dilemmas, making his task both rewarding and increasingly intricate. The decision ahead weighed heavily on Joseph's mind. Continuing meant delving deeper into Marlon's memories, possibly unraveling more complexities and adding layers to the already intricate story. It involved a risk – the possibility of things becoming more tangled, affecting not only Marlon but everyone connected to these memories.

On the other hand, pausing meant taking a step back to assess the potential consequences, contemplating how these revelations might shape Marlon's life and impact the broader circle of people tied to these past events. It was a balancing act between pursuing the truth and considering the potential disruptions that truth might bring.

It was like being caught between two big responsibilities: revealing everything truthfully and considering the feelings of everyone tied to these memories. Each detail brought this inner conflict, a battle between honesty and the emotions of others.

He wanted to be honest, to paint the whole picture, but at the same time, he didn't want to hurt anyone or cause more pain. Joseph had to tread carefully, thinking about how the truth could stir up emotions and yet hold onto the integrity of the story.

Striking that balance was like walking on a tightrope, trying not to sway too far one way or the other.

Each path he considered seemed fraught with challenges, uncertainties, and consequences. It was like standing amidst a maze with multiple directions, unsure which route to take. On one hand, he felt the urge to forge ahead, driven by the quest for truth buried within those memories. Yet, on the other hand, there was a nagging thought about the impact of his actions on the emotions and morals of those connected to the past he was unraveling.

Joseph grappled with the dilemma of whether to prioritize uncovering the truth or pause to consider the potential emotional and ethical ramifications of his endeavors. It was akin to being at a crossroads, contemplating which way to tread without causing unintended harm or upheaval.

The conflicting options weighed heavily on him, resembling a fierce tempest pulling in two opposing directions. On one hand, there was the urge to continue delving deeper into the memory narrative, to persist in uncovering the tale. But on the other hand, there lingered the need to pause, to step back and deeply contemplate the path forward. The decision he faced resembled an intricate riddle, with no obvious solution presenting itself. It was akin to standing at a crossroads, where both directions held uncertainty, leaving him grappling with the challenge of choosing the most prudent course without knowing its ultimate consequences. He was standing at the center of a maze, trying to figure out which way to go next. It's like a complicated map where every turn leads to something different, each path holding its own set of surprises and challenges.

He knows that the choice he makes isn't just about finding the way out of this maze of memories—it's about deciding the fate of Marlon's story and how it all fits with his own role in this journey through the past.

Joseph feels like he's on the edge, caught between his feelings and the huge responsibility on his shoulders. He's the one piecing together this story, trying to connect all the bits and make sense of everything.

But with that role comes a heap of thoughts swirling in his head, making him think hard about what might happen because of the choices he's about to make. He's not just considering Marlon's life but also how this journey could affect everyone else tangled up in these memories.

Every choice Joseph makes as a pebble thrown into a quiet pond, creating ripples that reach far and wide.

Each decision isn't just a single action—it's like setting off a chain reaction that travels back in time, affecting the lives of everyone involved in Marlon's story. It's as if Joseph is walking into uncharted territory with every move he makes, not knowing how these actions might reverberate through the intertwined lives woven within the memories. Each step forward feels heavy, carrying the possibility of changing the course of these interconnected destinies. Joseph is aware that his decisions might have lasting consequences, altering the past in ways that could echo through the lives of those connected to these memories. It's a daunting responsibility, considering how his choices might reshape the intricate web of lives embedded in Marlon's story.

Joseph felt the immense pressure of making the right decision, as if he was carrying a colossal mountain of responsibility on his shoulders.

The choice ahead of him wasn't just about picking a path; it was about how the future would unfold for Marlon and everyone connected to him. Each option seemed promising, like a welcoming road stretching ahead, but Joseph couldn't ignore the hidden uncertainties and the potential for unforeseen results lurking behind each choice. The weight of this decision wasn't just heavy; it was monumental, as it held the power to not only reshape the narrative but also profoundly impact the lives of everyone involved in ways he couldn't predict.

This choice wasn't just about the next step in unraveling memories; it was a clash between his fundamental values and the responsibilities weighing heavily on him. The paths ahead represented more than just routes through memories; they held the power to define Joseph's role in the lives intertwined within Marlon's intricate web of recollections.

Whatever choice he made would mark not only the end of this narrative but also determine the impact he'd have on the individuals navigating through the labyrinth of memories. It was a moment where his decision could shape destinies.

Chapter 16

The Weight of Responsibility

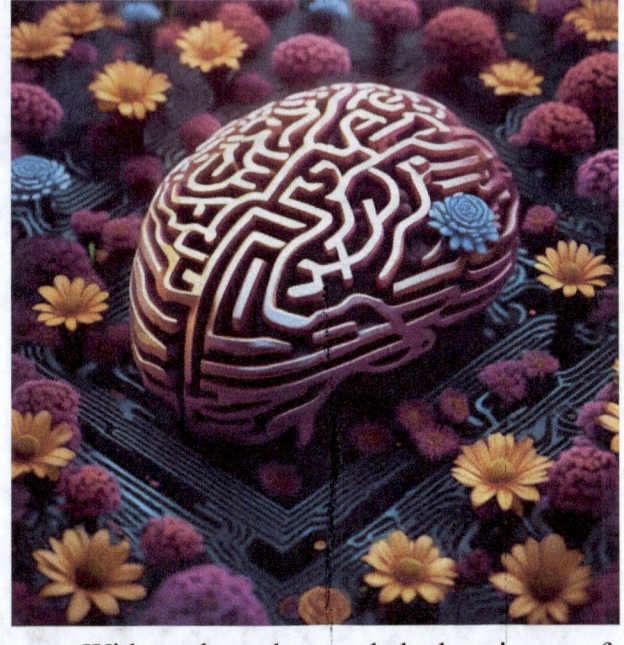

Joseph's journey into Marlon's memories was a mix of contrasting feelings. There were moments of clarity and confusion, lightness and heaviness. Each step deeper felt like lugging a heavy suitcase filled with memories. As he uncovered more pieces of the past, it added weight to his responsibility. With every new memory fragment, Joseph felt this added pressure to navigate the unfolding story with care. It wasn't just about unearthing moments; it was about handling them delicately, respecting their significance. These discoveries weren't merely puzzles to solve; they were laden with implications, prompting Joseph to confront tough choices and ponder deeply about the impact of each revelation. He found himself amidst a web of memories where scattered truths emerged, shedding light on past events. With each truth revealed, the picture of the past became clearer, yet it also brought a weightiness to the situation.

These revelations, though enlightening, came with a heavy load of responsibilities for Joseph. Every twist in the story and each new memory fragment stirred powerful emotions within him. While these discoveries brought understanding, they also posed challenges, making it tough for Joseph to grapple with the potential consequences of his actions and the impact they might have on the lives intertwined with these memories.

As Joseph continued unraveling the memories, it wasn't just information or thoughts; it was as if reality itself was surfacing, vivid and impactful. The weight of these revelations was immense—they felt substantial, like they held the power to turn lives upside down. With each new piece of insight, it was a stark reminder of the enormity of the truths he unearthed. These weren't just bits of history; they held the potential to cause seismic shifts in Marlon's life and ripple out to affect everyone connected to his tale.

It was a realization that what he discovered wasn't merely knowledge but something deeply profound and potentially life-altering for many.

The weight of responsibility pressing on Joseph's shoulders felt like carrying something massive. He

was caught in a tough spot, feeling pulled in two directions. On one side, there was this strong urge to uncover the truth buried within those memories. But on the other side, he couldn't shake off the worry about how his actions might affect the people linked to those memories. Each step he took felt like a battle inside him, a fight between his quest for truth and his concern for everyone's safety. It was like being at a crossroads, torn between two equally significant but conflicting paths. The struggle within him intensified with every decision, making it harder to balance the quest for truth with the well-being of those involved.

What began as a task to piece together memories had evolved into something weightier. He felt this inner conflict between his thirst for complete understanding and his desire to shield the emotions and peace of those whose stories were surfacing. It felt like being at a crossroads, torn between unveiling every detail and safeguarding the emotional sanctity of those involved.

He grappled with the tension between pursuing truth and preserving the serenity of others, as if standing between two diverging paths, trying to find a balance between unraveling the story and ensuring the emotional well-being of everyone linked to it.

This delicate balance became the crux of his dilemma, impacting the way he moved forward in his exploration of these memories. The path ahead seemed unclear, with two diverging roads, each leading to different outcomes.

Moving forward might cause a cascade of unforeseen events, potentially altering the lives of everyone tied to these memories. And pausing or stepping back could mean sacrificing vital truths and fairness in understanding the past.

The gravity of his decision loomed large, as every choice he made had the potential to significantly impact the lives and perceptions of those involved in this complex web of memories.

The dilemma was immense, forcing him to navigate between the risks of uncertainty and the necessity for completeness and fairness. Each thread of truth seemed interwoven with the potential to disrupt or heal, to unravel the existing harmony or stitch together broken fragments.

He grappled with the role of being the custodian of intertwined narratives, knowing their power to

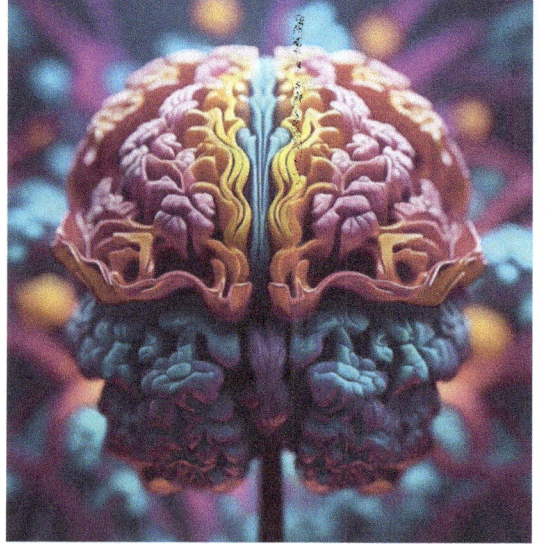

mend or shatter.

The weight of responsibility, not merely a burden on his mind but on his very essence, tugged at him. Every decision felt like a stone dropped into a pond, sending ripples far beyond himself, impacting the lives of those connected to these stories.

It wasn't just about his actions; it was about their collective repercussions. The enormity of this responsibility transcended personal choices, becoming a shared journey tied to the fate of others. The desire to unveil the reality clashed with the fear of potential repercussions. Each new discovery felt like a sharp pang, a reminder of the precarious situation he navigated.

There was this intense longing to do what felt right, to shed light on the reality, but at the same time, an overwhelming concern about the aftermath loomed large.

He was akin to being ensnared in a dilemma, torn between the yearning to act and the dread of the unknown aftermath. The conflicting forces trapped him in a state of paralysis, immobilized by the uncertainty of the outcomes while battling the urge to take action aligned with his convictions. He felt like standing at a pivotal moment, a crossroads that carried immense weight, as the choices ahead held the power to shape the stories and lives connected to them.

At this critical juncture, Joseph grappled with a significant burden of responsibility. His aim was to tread carefully, ensuring that his decisions honored two fundamental aspects: the truth embedded within the memories and the care he owed to the individuals whose lives were intricately woven into these memories.

He aimed for equilibrium, seeking to preserve the integrity of the truth while delicately navigating the complexities of empathy and responsibility.

The challenge lay in maintaining the authenticity of the memories while safeguarding the dignity and emotions of those involved. Joseph understood the need to handle this intricate balance with the utmost care, respecting the narratives of the past while acknowledging the impact his choices might have on the present and future.

Chapter 17

The Inner Conflict

In the whirlwind of heavy responsibilities and important choices, Joseph felt like he was engulfed in a powerful storm brewing within him. It was as if a tempest of thoughts, doubts, and uncertainties raged through his mind, clouding his ability to think clearly.

The weight of his decisions felt immense, pressing down on him like a thick fog, obscuring his path forward. Every choice he contemplated seemed shrouded in uncertainty, leaving him hesitant and unsure about the best course of action. It was like being in a place where every turn led to more confusion, making it challenging to discern the right direction amidst the chaos.

Joseph's involvement in unraveling memories felt like a weight pressing down on his heart.

The impact of his actions on Marlon's life and the interconnected individuals felt like looming shadows, casting a cloud over his mind and unsettling his peace. He recognized that his task resembled piecing together a puzzle, but the pieces didn't fit seamlessly. It created a tangled web of information, making it challenging to make sense of and organize the complexities of the situation. The emotional burden Joseph carried was significant; he felt the gravity of the implications that every decision might have on those involved. It was akin to sorting through a jigsaw puzzle with mismatched pieces, trying to decipher a coherent picture from elements that didn't align neatly.

This sense of disarray added to the strain he felt, making the task both mentally taxing and emotionally distressing, a complex situation, leaving him uncertain about the right course of action, especially considering his role in documenting memories.

Amidst this turmoil, he delved deep within himself, contemplating the potential impact of his actions and the significant repercussions they might bring about. His mind was inundated with profound inquiries. Joseph grappled with the extent to which his interventions altered the lives of those connected to the memories he worked with. He yearned to comprehend the direct consequences of his involvement and how it had shaped the experiences and destinies of the individuals linked to these recollections. The weight of these unanswered questions weighed heavily on his conscience as he sought to navigate the moral and ethical implications of his work.

His involvement with memories weighed heavily on him, resonating deeper than he initially comprehended. This realization troubled him, stirring concerns that he might have overstepped a boundary that was meant to maintain a clear separation between his duty and the emotional ties people held with those memories.

The thick fog of uncertainty created an unsettling environment, leaving Joseph feeling unsure about the impact of his actions. He questioned whether his engagement with these memories went beyond its intended scope, blurring the line between his professional responsibilities and the emotions tethered to those recollections.

This inner conflict amplified his apprehensions, raising doubts about the boundaries he might have crossed in his pursuit of unraveling the past. Each decision seemed obscured by uncertainty, akin to navigating through a landscape where clarity was elusive. His actions with the memories only seemed to compound the complexity, adding more layers to an already enigmatic narrative, fueling a fire of endless questions without offering any resolution. Like a lone sailor in a tempest, Joseph grappled with these challenges solo, seeking a way to harmonize his professional duty with his emotional compass.

He yearned for a guiding light, something to illuminate the path toward a balance between truth-telling and safeguarding the emotional impact of those memories on others. It was akin to seeking equilibrium between the authenticity of the narrative and the preservation of individuals' sentiments intertwined with those recollections.

It was as if he was in an unending quest for solutions, yet they remained elusive and hard to grasp. At times, there was an overwhelming urge to continue with his responsibilities, but conflicting moments emerged when he felt the need to pause and deeply reflect on the situation. His primary concern lay in ensuring the authenticity of the memories, aiming to uphold the truth. Simultaneously, he was equally devoted to safeguarding the emotional well-being of those intertwined with these recollections, wanting to ensure their sentiments were respected and protected. Striking this delicate balance between truthfulness and emotional consideration posed a constant challenge for him.

The conflict between what he deemed right and the consideration for people's emotions created a tumultuous terrain within him. His uncertainty about the next steps mirrored a feeling of being trapped in a maze, where tasks and challenges intertwined, making the path forward unclear. Amidst this chaos, his primary desire was to regain a sense of inner peace. The complexity of the situation left him yearning for clarity, particularly because his actions seemed to complicate matters rather than resolve them. The disarray caused by the decisions he made amplified his quest for tranquility and resolution.

Chapter **18**

The Threshold
of Revelation

It was a pivotal moment where every decision Joseph made held the power to shape the unfolding narrative significantly. Aware of the profound impact of his actions, Joseph realized that his choices carried weight, affecting everyone associated with these memories. As he delved deeper into Marlon's recollections, each fragment added to the intricate puzzle weighed heavily on him. The complexity of the story he was unraveling felt like a vast tapestry woven with Marlon's emotions and the experiences of all those intertwined in his life. With each added piece, Joseph sensed the increasing gravity of the situation, as if the weight of this responsibility rested squarely on his shoulders.

Joseph's journey through these discoveries was akin to finding puzzle pieces that seemed to fit the truth, yet with each piece, the picture grew more intricate and perplexing.

This sense of revelation brought both clarity and a fog of uncertainty. The weight of responsibility rested heavily on Joseph's shoulders, bearing the gravity of the choices ahead.

He understood the magnitude of these decisions, realizing that each step carried immense significance, capable of reshaping the entire landscape of the unfolding narrative.

The path he chose wasn't just a single step but a catalyst for a cascade of consequences, making each decision a pivotal moment with far-reaching implications.

On one side, there was this strong pull to unravel the story completely, to connect all the dots and reveal the whole truth. It felt like an essential task, piecing together every fragment to understand the narrative fully. Yet, on the other side, there loomed a cautionary voice, warning him of the potential consequences.

It was as if uncovering everything might lead to serious repercussions, stirring up trouble or causing harm in some way. The dilemma was between seeking total clarity and heeding the warning of potential negative outcomes tied to the complete revelation of the story.

There was this intense urge to connect the dots, to assemble every fragment of memory into a complete narrative. He was driven by this fervent curiosity to uncover the truth, to understand the whole story behind the memories. However, there was also this heavy weight of caution tugging at him, warning of potential consequences if he uncovered everything. This caution made him hesitate, causing him to pause and reconsider.

It was a back-and-forth struggle between the desire for

clarity and the fear of potential fallout if the whole truth was revealed. Joseph was caught in this whirlpool of wanting to know but also worrying about the consequences that might follow the complete revelation.

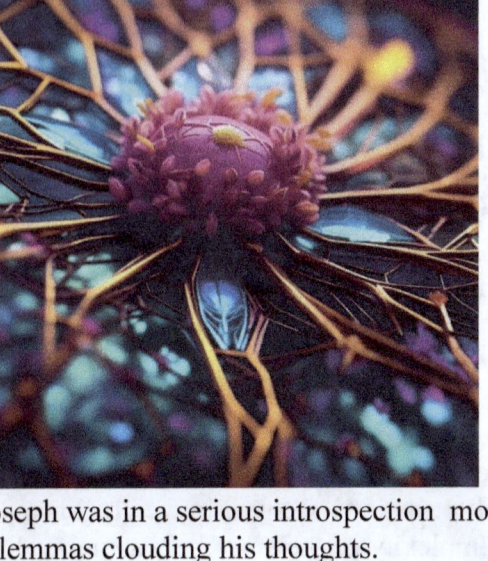

He know that his actions regarding the memories held immense power. There was this pressing need to reveal everything, to be transparent about Marlon's past, and piece together the complete story, and there was this equally strong pull to protect those intertwined with those memories.

It felt like balancing on a tightrope, where one wrong step could cause an imbalance, potentially causing harm to those whose lives were entangled in Marlon's past.

Joseph grappled with the conflict between his duty to unearth the truth and the responsibility to safeguard the emotions and safety of everyone involved, teetering between transparency and discretion to ensure both honesty and security in handling Marlon's memories.

Joseph was in a serious introspection mode, diving into the depths of his mind, trying to sort out the dilemmas clouding his thoughts.

The weight of his decisions felt immense; it was like each choice he made held the power to reshape the lives of those intertwined in the memories he handled. It was as if the decisions he grappled with weren't just simple choices but pivotal moments that could rewrite the entire narrative for everyone involved.

He realized that his actions weren't isolated; they were threads woven into the fabric of others' lives, influencing their stories in significant ways.

This realization made every decision feel monumental, laden with the potential to significantly impact the interconnected lives tied to those memories.

There was an intense concern, a worry that weighed heavily on him, making him cautious and hesitant. Simultaneously, there was an unwavering focus, a determination pushing him to uncover the truth buried within the memories. This internal conflict created a deep sense of apprehension.

He desired to unravel the truth, to piece together the fragments of the story, yet the fear of potential repercussions loomed large. It was as if he stood at a precipice, teetering on the brink of a decision that could alter the entire narrative, profoundly impacting the lives intertwined with the memories he was unraveling.

The memories he delved into were like a collage of intertwined fragments, each beckoning for attention yet clouded in ambiguity. As he navigated through these recollections, the responsibility of crafting this narrative weighed heavily on him. Every small detail he unearthed felt critical, as if he was walking a tightrope, wary not to disrupt the delicate balance, afraid of the potential repercussions that might unfold from his actions.

It was akin to walking on eggshells, trying hard not to make a misstep that could have far-reaching consequences he couldn't predict.

Joseph had this intense desire to uncover every truth hidden within the memories, piecing together the complete story. However, there was this nagging worry about how revealing the truth might impact the lives of those connected to it. It was as if he stood at the precipice, torn between divulging everything and safeguarding everyone involved.

At that moment, Joseph's mind was in overdrive, consumed by deep contemplation. The distinction between what was right and what wasn't became a bit fuzzy due to the immense responsibility he carried.

The weight of his choices was so heavy that it clouded the clarity he needed to discern the best course of action. He was trying to navigate the intricate balance between seeking truth and ensuring the safety and well-being of those intertwined in these memories.

He was in the middle of deciding what's more important: telling everything true or keeping people safe who were connected to that truth.

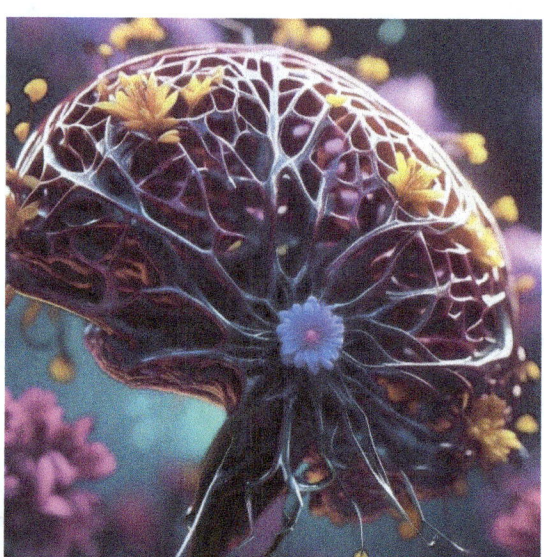

Chapter 19

The Harvest of Truth

As Joseph revealed all the memories and untangled the threads of the story, it felt like a colossal storm had swept through. The emotions, truths, and perspectives that had been hidden or obscured were suddenly brought to light. It was as if this storm had cleared away the debris, making everything about the story vivid and complete in a way it hadn't been before. The bigger picture became visible— each memory fragment, like a puzzle piece, fell into place, painting a clearer, more comprehensive image. With the unveiling of these memories, the story transformed, unveiling truths and emotions that had been concealed, ultimately reshaping how everyone involved perceived the entire narrative.

He's been dedicating himself tirelessly, investing immense time and energy into piecing together Marlon's memories, treating it like a monumental puzzle.

With meticulous care and unwavering patience, he's been aligning each fragment, but the enormity of the complete picture catches him off guard. It's a pivotal moment, flooding him with a surge of emotions he never anticipated. Each memory he's curated, delicately placed like bricks in a wall, suddenly unveils a grandeur beyond his anticipation. This unexpected magnitude hits him like a wave, realizing the depth and significance of the memories he's been assembling. This revelation is akin to standing in the midst of a grand painting, working tirelessly on individual strokes only to step back and witness the masterpiece in its entirety, overwhelming him with its sheer magnitude and emotional weight.

Every tiny discovery, each memory he carefully examines, contributes to a significant realization brewing on the horizon. It's akin to assembling a jigsaw puzzle, diligently piecing together fragments, only to witness a breathtaking picture that redefines his entire perception.

This revelation isn't just a tweak to what he knew before; it's a seismic shift, reshaping his core beliefs and emotions.

The truth he uncovers isn't merely a change of facts; it's an emotional whirlwind, like hurtling through loops and twists on a roller coaster ride.

It throws surprises at him, sparks amazement, and triggers deep contemplation about everything he thought he understood. Joseph's not the only one feeling this way. Everyone connected to these memories is in the same boat. When the complete truth comes out from these memories, it's like a big storm for them too. It totally changes how they see things, shaking up their lives and what they thought they knew about the past. All the things they were so sure about before are now unclear, and they're faced with a reality that's both puzzling and eye-opening.

Discovering the truth can be like a sudden thunderclap on a sunny day, rattling everyone's emotions. It's not just about being surprised; it's an avalanche of feelings—shock, wonder, sadness, and sometimes even a glimmer of hope. This whirlwind of emotions catches everyone off guard, shaking their world like an unexpected storm. Imagine it as a turning point, abruptly altering the path they thought they were on.

Suddenly, they're confronted with questions about what they believed and the actions they took based on those beliefs.

It's a moment that flips their understanding upside down, forcing them to reassess everything they thought they knew. Discovering a hidden truth is like turning on a light in a dark room, suddenly revealing details that were hidden before. Imagine everyone involved in a story, thinking they understood it all, but then, boom! The truth hits them like a surprise wave.

It's as if they're seeing their reflection in a mirror they've never looked into before, noticing new angles and details they never imagined. This sudden realization flips their world upside down. It's not just a tiny revelation; it's like the ground beneath their feet shifting entirely. They're forced to reevaluate everything they thought they knew, reconsidering their actions, thoughts, and their place in the bigger picture. The truth reshapes their understanding, challenging their beliefs in ways they never anticipated.

When something big happens that changes everything, it's like a switch gets flipped inside people's minds. Imagine you're in a room filled with old furniture, and suddenly, a gust of wind rearranges everything. That's what happens when a revelation hits. People start diving into their own thoughts, digging deep into their memories like treasure hunters looking for clues. It's like rewinding a movie and rewatching every scene from a new angle.

They're reflecting on the past, questioning their choices, and sorting through their emotions like someone going through an old chest of belongings.

It's a moment of stepping back, looking at the intricate connections between each other, and trying to make sense of a complex situation that seemed straightforward before.

When a big truth comes out, it's like turning on a powerful spotlight in a room filled with shadows. Suddenly, everything becomes clear, but along with that clarity comes a wave of mixed emotions. Imagine being in a room where you thought you knew where everything was, but suddenly the furniture rearranges itself. That's what happens with this revelation. It's a moment that shakes up everything people believed, making them reconsider their place in this intricate puzzle of memories. This truth unravels the story they thought they understood, leading them to question their own roles and connections to this complex tale.

Chapter 20

The Gardens
of Destiny

Joseph finds himself in an incredibly challenging mental state. His responsibility as a memory shaper weighs heavily on him, feeling like a burden that's hard to shake off. He's stuck in a whirlwind of thoughts, trying to navigate the ethical divide of working with memories. On one side, he sees the immense impact his actions have had, altering numerous lives and leaving him grappling with the fallout. He's wrestling with the implications of delving into memories, torn between the desire to uncover truths and the potential repercussions it brings to those involved. This inner struggle has left him feeling caught between his responsibilities and the moral complexities of his role as a memory worker, unsure of the best path forward. He is facing a colossal challenge at this stage of his journey, akin to scaling an enormous mountain.

With every piece of the past he uncovers, the weight of responsibility grows heavier on his shoulders. He's starting to grasp the enormity of the impact his actions might have had and the secrets he's unraveled. It's like paving a new path that's about to drastically alter the course of Marlon's life and the lives o f everyone intertwined with him. Each revelation adds to this evolving road, leading toward an uncertain future, and Joseph is becoming acutely aware of the magnitude of influence his discoveries might wield on their destinies. Joseph finds himself overwhelmed with emotions as he reflects on the impact of his actions on everyone connected to these memories. It's a tricky situation for him; he's navigating the fine line between the incredible power of altering memories and the delicate, precarious nature of doing so. It's like holding onto something immensely potent, yet incredibly fragile, all at the same time.

He grapples with the weight of responsibility that comes with his role—realizing that while he can influence the past through memories, any alterations could have unforeseen consequences, affecting not just the present but also the future of those involved. This dichotomy of power and fragility leaves him in a state of deep contemplation, weighing the risks against the potential changes he could bring about.

As Joseph nears the conclusion of his journey, he starts to reflect deeply on all the experiences he's had. He's learned a lot, especially about the fragility of memories and their incredible impact on people's lives. Memories, he realizes, are delicate, like fragile glass ornaments, yet they hold immense power. They serve as a bridge, connecting individuals to what they've lost or forgotten, rekindling emotions and experiences that might have faded with time.

Even though dealing with memories can be complex and evoke a whirlwind of emotions, he recognizes their significance in helping individuals reconnect with their past, bringing solace, understanding, and a sense of belonging, no matter how tangled or intricate they might be.

At the journey's close, Joseph finds himself in a garden of memories, a place lush with the growth and bloom of experiences. It's akin to a tranquil space where he reflects on his entire voyage. In this garden, memories are like seeds planted long ago, now flourishing into vibrant flowers. Each memory holds a unique story, representing lives that have been touched and transformed by Joseph's actions and choices. These memories have taken root and blossomed, illustrating the profound impact of his work. As he gazes upon this garden, he sees not just the moments he's shaped, but the lives that have been nurtured and changed by the careful tending of these memories.

In this moment of reflection, Joseph takes a deep dive into his own thoughts and feelings. He's acknowledging a lot of significant ideas. Firstly, he's understanding the profound impact memories have on individuals; how these recollections can shape and transform people's lives, sometimes in unexpected ways. He's realized the importance of reconstructing memories, how it's like putting together pieces of a complex puzzle, intricate and challenging. But despite its complexity, he's come to terms with the fact that his work is profoundly meaningful. Joseph feels a sense of contentment, knowing that his efforts have helped people uncover truths buried within their memories, allowing them to heal and move forward. He recognizes the value in this act of guiding people toward a better understanding of their own pasts.

Joseph stands in this remarkable space he has cultivated, akin to a garden where his tireless work has bloomed into something extraordinary.

The gardens here symbolize so much more than just memories; they're a testament to the stories and lives Joseph has touched and helped nurture. Each flower and plant echoes the narratives of the individuals he's guided and supported through their memory journeys. It's like these gardens whisper tales of resilience and growth, signifying new beginnings for those who once grappled with their pasts. Joseph's efforts have become a beacon of hope, portraying that despite the journey ending, the impact will linger on. These gardens will serve as a lasting legacy, aiding people in embracing and reconciling with their histories, weaving them seamlessly into their present lives in a positive and enriching manner. Joseph is at a really important moment, standing on the edge of what's happened because of his work with memories. He's thinking deeply about what his actions have led to and what they've meant for the people he's been helping.

There's this big weight on his mind, realizing that uncovering the truth he sought came with some serious changes.

While he was trying to do the right thing, he understands that by digging into these memories, he's altered the lives of those who relied on him. It's like he's balancing between knowing he did something important and feeling the weight of how it's impacted everyone else involved.

Joseph's seeing the aftermath of the truth he uncovered, how it's affected Marlon and everyone connected to this whole journey through memories. He's realizing how big this change is for them, how their lives are different now because of what they've learned. It's like a heavy weight on Joseph's shoulders, knowing that what he did has caused some big shifts in their lives. But despite this weight, he's finding comfort in being there for them.

He was like a light in the darkness, helping them find the truth, even if it was hard. He's seeing that sometimes facing painful truths is the only way to move forward, and being that guide means a lot to him. The gardens at the end of Joseph's journey are like a beautiful picture of how everyone's changed and grown.

Each flower in the garden represents a person whose life has changed because of what happened. The leaves symbolize new understandings, like how they've come to know things they didn't before. The roots show how they've reconnected to their past in a different way. Joseph realizes that these changes wouldn't have happened without his help. He sees his role as super important in helping everyone find out the truth and make peace with it. It's like the gardens hold the stories of everyone he's supported, and it's a really powerful and meaningful sight for him.

Joseph says goodbye to this part of his life feeling like everything's complete and clear. He knows he's shared memories and truths, but what happens next with these memories, how they grow and what they mean, that's up to the people who now have them. His job of working with memories is finished, and it's like he's left behind a lot of truth and understanding for people to use in their lives. He feels like a farmer who's planted seeds of truth, and now they've grown into something that belongs to everyone, like a big garden full of li fe lessons and understanding.